GROUSE FEATHERS

Grouse Feathers

BY BURTON L. SPILLER

ILLUSTRATED BY

LYNN BOGUE HUNT

Introduction by H. G. Tapply

CROWN PUBLISHERS, INC., NEW YORK

© 1972 by Burton L. Spiller
Library of Congress Catalog Card Number: 72-85577
ISBN: 0-517-50085X
Printed in the United States of America
Published simultaneously in Canada by
General Publishing Company Limited

TO THAT VAST MULTITUDE
OF SCATTER-GUN ENTHUSIASTS
TO WHOM
THE THUNDER OF RISING GROUSE
IS A LORELEI
AND THE WHISTLE OF WOODCOCK
A SIREN SONG
THIS BOOK IS DEDICATED

INTRODUCTION

Grouse shooting in my "Spiller covers" very nearly touched bottom last fall. A hard day's hunt with an industrious dog might get a half-dozen birds into the air, on the average: wild, edgy birds that flushed too far out for a shot more often than not and seldom offered a chance for a second start—and this in once-prime New Hampshire grouse country where in times not long past it was commonplace to move from thirty to fifty grouse a day.

To one who lifts his highball glass and notes that it is still half-full, rather than half-empty, this may not seem cause for great alarm. Grouse populations have always fluctuated, and the fall of '71 may have only marked the low point of another cycle here in New England. I'm told there was a veritable glut of grouse in Minnesota last fall, so perhaps they will make another comeback here, too.

But I tend to doubt it. Looking back over the years I've hunted grouse, nearly four decades now, it seems to me that each high point in the cycle has not been quite so high as the previous one—and each low point has been a little lower. That isn't to say that the grouse *couldn't* come back, given the chance. No species of wildlife is hardier, none better able to survive heavy shooting, predation, or the bitter winds of winter. But I do know they will never return to our Old Schoolhouse Cover, because a power line cuts through it now, or to many other "birdy" places of yesteryear where the old apple orchards and wild grape tangles have been bulldozed away to make room for more houses and more sterile ribbons of macadam.

So I contemplate my highball glass and think morosely that grouse shooting here in New England may be half-gone too, and there's no possible way to get a refill.

If that is so, then it becomes important that we have a record of what New England grouse shooting was like in its day of glory . . . and no one ever knew it better, or wrote about it with greater eloquence, than my old friend and gunning partner Burton L. Spiller.

[v]

Burt was lucky. He was born at the right time and in the right place, among the abandoned New England farmlands when they were growing wild and creating an idyllic habitat for grouse. Ever since he became old enough to lift a shotgun to his shoulder Burt had grouse to hunt, grouse almost everywhere he went, in every orchard edge and alder run and strip lot, grouse in singles, pairs, and family broods, and always plenty of birds left over at season's end to seed the covers for another year. During the autumn months he hunted four, five, six days a week, year after year, into the season of 1964, when he reluctantly concluded that an old geezer of seventy-seven had better start taking things a little easier. In November of that year he oiled and racked his shotgun for the last time.

That might be the end of it, except that sometime along the way, back in the early thirties, Burt began writing about his lifelong love affair with the New England pa'tridge. He scribbled evenings till long into the night, trying to put on paper the feelings he had about grouse and about the men and dogs who hunted them. Although untrained as a writer and largely self-educated, he nevertheless wrote easily and with rare eloquence, and it is not surprising, knowing what we know now, that Ray Holland, then editor of *Field & Stream* magazine, bought and published the first story Burt wrote—titled, aptly enough, "His Majesty, the Grouse"—or that Ray and his successors at *Field & Stream* have printed more than half a hundred of Burt's stories since then.

It was during this time that Burt began to think about writing a book. He played with the idea awhile and began setting his words on paper, a labor of love in its most literal sense. When he finished the manuscript, late in 1934, he addressed the package to Eugene V. Connett, then publisher of Derrydale Press in New York, and in 1935 *Grouse Feathers* was printed in a deluxe limited edition of 950 numbered copies at $10 each.

It would be hard to guess who was the happier about the success of their venture, Connett or Spiller. In any event, both were greatly encouraged by it, obviously, for in the following year they brought forth a second book, *Thoroughbred,* and the next year *Firelight,* and the year after that, *More Grouse Feathers.* To this day all are prized collector's items, although *Grouse Feathers* and *More Grouse Feathers* are the better known and most sought after. When a copy of either becomes available from a dealer in old books, the price ranges from $90 to $100, with plenty of buyers eager to snap up the bargain.

In 1947 The Macmillan Company republished *Grouse Feathers* in a facsimile edition, but for some reason I can't guess at—perhaps my old friend was temporarily in limbo, or there were still a few second-hand copies of the Derrydale edition to be had—it soon disappeared from the bookstores.

During the past twenty-five years interest in Burt Spiller's writings has revived, as interest in grouse shooting seems to have freshened too, despite my gloomy forebodings about the future of the sport here in New England. Within just the past couple of years William Harnden Foster's *New England Grouse Shooting* has been republished, and Frank Woolner's *Grouse and Grouse Shooting* has met with the success it so richly deserves.

So Burt must be right: so long as there is an undisturbed corner bounded by walls of gray New Hampshire stone, with a few old apple trees still bearing wizened fruit and a clump of pines nearby for shelter during storms, there will be grouse to hunt in New England, and men and dogs to hunt them.

So now it is time again for the first of the great grouse-shooting classics. Gentlemen and fellow wanderers of the autumn uplands, I give you *Grouse Feathers.* May you find the same delight in its pages that I still do every time I read it.

H. G. TAPPLY

East Alton, New Hampshire
April 1972

GROUSE FEATHERS

CHAPTER I

I BELIEVE I had reached the rather impressive age of six when I bagged my first really big game.

As I recall it now, I think it was Sitting Bull who was my first victim. He had been raising Hades among the chaparral far too long to suit my youthful fancy and, when I saw him peering around the corner of the shed at me, with that sinister eye of his, I let him have it—"bing—bing—bing!" like that. No fuss, no bother, nothing even to wax lyric about. Just "bing—bing—bing!" and he was the proverbial good Indian.

It is with a faint glow of pride that I recall I was fast on the trigger even then. The fact that the gun was of wood, with no visible mechanism, seemed to be no disadvantage. It worked as smoothly as a present-day sub-machine gun, never varying a grain in powder charge, excepting on those rare occasions when it was necessary to administer the *coup de grace* to a supposedly dead victim. Then it said "BANG!" viciously, venomously, in a childish treble. One "BANG!" was usually sufficient for the most aggravating case.

But Indians were too ridiculously easy to bag and I sought a less vulnerable target. My *Chatterbox*, an English publication for children and imported for what reason I have never been able to determine, aroused in me the impression that bears were our only really dangerous game. Strange it is how those childish impressions still linger. Even now I hesitate to place a pop bottle between the paws of a bear I know to be perfectly tame and feel a tickling up and down my spine when his capable tongue extracts a peanut from between my fingers.

So I started in to rid our community of bears, with all the enthusiasm of a vice squad embarking on a campaign to clean up a city. I believe, however, that of the two, my undertaking was crowned with the greater success, for I am informed, on good authority, that no wild bears have roamed the streets of that suburban village since those days of slaughter and carnage in the latter part of the last century.

It must have been in my seventh year that the consciousness dawned upon me that grouse were a factor to be considered. Dad was a grouse hunter—when he could play truant from business—and I recall certain savory stews which may have helped to mould my childish opinion. Here was something tangible, a separate entity emerging from the phantasmagoria of my childish imagination. A thing that lived, that moved, that was possessed—according to Dad—with uncanny cunning, with lightning swiftness awing, with the power of becoming invisible at will or of shaping its mobile body to the perfect image of a stick or stone. A thing to be desired above all things else.

In my imagination, I placed him upon a jeweled pedestal and crowned him King. There, after nearly forty years, he still sits, his throne unchallenged, his glory undimmed by the passage of time.

Then, in the fall of my eighth year, Dad took me with him, for a glorious month, into the wilds of Maine. We explored the Dead River country and there I made associations which call me back periodically. Stately old Mount Bigelow, so closely allied with Arnold's ill-fated expedition, Saddleback, Kennebago, the Rangeleys. Today that country is still a sportsman's paradise and I, O lucky little me, fished and hunted there with Dad almost forty years ago.

Looking backward, from the vantage point of years, I am led to believe that this excursion had much to do with the shaping of my destiny. For a long time I wondered why Dad burdened himself with me. I must have been an incumbrance, for I was very young. But in my later years I have come to believe I know the answer. Good, kindly old Dad must have sensed, even then, he would have little of worldly wealth to bestow upon his children and was farseeing enough to teach us to love the better things of life—the great, God-given out-of-doors, good literature, good music and good sportsmanship.

Thank you, Dad.

[3]

Much of that wonderful month has gone from my memory but other things stand out as clearly as though they happened yesterday. I believe we had our headquarters at a farmhouse, for I have a hazy recollection of eating at a long table at which other people sat, but vividly clear is the remembrance of those times we sat before the campfire, with the friendly night closing down and the first stars peeping out at us. There were trout sizzling in the frying pan and sweet corn roasting in the coals. One could hardly expect a kid of eight to forget that, could they?

I remember, also, a great concourse of people assembled before a large old house around which spread a vast expanse of velvety turf. Whether it was a picnic, a town holiday or some calamity, like a wedding, which drew the people together, I have not the faintest idea but I do remember the sudden cessation of laughter and movement in the group as all eyes turned toward the woods, some distance away.

Two men had entered the clearing and were coming toward us. They were carrying axes in their hands and rifles on their shoulders. They entered our group and we gathered about them. They had been setting bear traps and had seen the tracks of a truly enormous bear. They would have him in less than a week, they assured us. Someone in the crowd displayed interest in one of the rifles and inquired the make.

"That's a Colt, 44, slide action," said the guide.

"Is it loaded?"

"No. There's some in the magazine, though."

"May I look at it?"

"Sure."

I remember the man taking it, turning it over, admiringly in his hands, placing it carefully against his shoulder and looking long and earnestly through the sights. Then, while those who should have known stood speechless, he slid the action open and shut and, with the gun pointing directly through the crowd, pulled the trigger.

Distinctly I recall that bellowing "POW!" and the belching powder smoke, the startled cries, the shaking hands of the man with the gun. Memory fails to record the next few minutes but I remember, after that, a man walking about among the group, displaying a coat which had a ragged cut, about ten inches long, across the back.

"It never touched me," he explained, "but look what it did to my coat."

I hope the incident proved to be a lesson to the chap who pulled the trigger. It was to me, nor have I forgotten it through the years.

It was on this expedition that I saw my first grouse. I was trudging along behind Dad when there came a sudden thunder of wings beside us and a grouse hammered up through the birches with the speed of a rocket. In the instant that he cleared their tops, Dad's gun roared, deafeningly, and my eyes, glued to that hurtling form, saw it collapse, lifeless, in mid-air. It was a clean, fast kill, deceptive in its smoothness, and the effortless ease of it fooled me.

"I'll bet I could do that," I boasted.

Dad grinned.

"I hope you will, some day," he said.

CHAPTER II

THE next spring we left the city of my nativity and moved some thirty miles away to a farm bordering on tidewater. That, too, had much to do with shaping my destiny for, after hunting over many hundreds of square miles, I know of no sweeter shooting grounds for upland game birds than those coverts within tramping distance of that little farm on the coast of Maine. Then, too, it had the added advantage of affording wonderful waterfowl shooting for there were countless acres of marshland and eelgrass beds. Here the ducks and geese came, literally in thousands, each spring and fall.

In those halcyon days an 8 gauge was considered the ideal duck gun and if, by chance, it had 34 inch barrels and weighed twelve pounds, it was a thing to weep with joy over, or to discuss with the neighbor you chanced to meet at the crossroads. It was not an uncommon thing to hear that "Sam Smith got sixteen black ducks with one bar'l last night," or that "Bill Jinkins let both bar'ls go into a flock of geese, down at the lower dike, an' got five of 'em." Ah, well! Men were men in those days.

Dad, however, was conservative. With a farm and large orchard to care for, and a bunch of livestock consisting of several cows and calves, a pair of horses, numberless hens, a litter of pigs—and seven children—two guns were an unaffordable luxury. So the little pa'tridge gun was sacrificed and an all 'round gun usurped its place over the kitchen mantel.

"A neat job," and "a darned nice handlin' little gun," the neighbors called it and I, gullible youth that I was, believed them. It was a 10 gauge, equipped with 30 inch barrels, and weighed a shade under nine pounds. I know now that it was a monstrosity, an instrument of torture suited admirably to the Spanish Inquisition but, for years, I argued its merits to all and sundry. I'll argue about it now, too, with anyone, till the crack of doom, for I grew up with Old Betsy for several years, tortured as to shoulder and with a nose that bled at the slightest touch. I learned her idiosyncrasies after a weary, weary while and respected them, but the fear of bodily harm, from anything smaller than a locomotive, had departed forever.

Well do I recall the first time I felt that vertebrae-breaking recoil. I had begged the privilege and, one day, Dad hoisted the thing up on a sawhorse, cocked one barrel and bade me go to it. I approached it, draped myself around the stock and felt for the trigger with much the same mental attitude of a boy taking his first, tentative poke at a hornets' nest; interested but not absolutely certain of the outcome.

Cautiously I hooked my finger about the trigger and

gave it a decided yank. The result was beautiful. I do not know all the things which happened but I am firmly convinced that whatever did happen, occurred without undue loss of time. It was tremendous, that recoil, but something was born in me, in that moment while I lay on my back in the barnyard litter, that has never yet been fully satisfied. I sat up and, as I tried to stanch my bleeding nose, asked, "Cad I shood id agaid?"

"You bet," said Dad, as he led me to the house. "Next Saturday."

Thus Saturdays became, in my youthful fancy, different than other days, and the delusion still lingers. It is an enchanted day. A day when, theoretically, all the grouse and woodcock in my hunting range are listening for my footsteps. During the open season I seldom disappoint them, no matter how much I may have hunted through the week.

Old Betsy became mine on Saturday mornings, contingent on my good behavior through the week. Never was barn work done more thoroughly or woodbox piled higher than was ours during the hunting season, and in those days that was long enough to delight the heart of almost any Nimrod.

Ducks and geese came back the first of April. Whether or not there was a law in those days prohibiting spring shooting I do not know, but everyone hunted them. I wish

[9]

we hadn't. It was a mistake and we should have discovered it long before we did.

Then, when the waterfowl were gone, the shore birds came in untold thousands—sandpipers, plover, curlew, yellow-legs. One could get enough for a meal for the whole family in a few hours. There were upland plover, too. A wonderful bird and plentiful enough for good shooting but, alas, I have almost forgotten how they looked for I have not seen one for many years.

With the coming of September the marshes became populated with teal. Here was duck shooting to delight the heart of anyone and to cause endless nights of discussion as to load and lead, for they were swift as an arrow in their flight.

September 15th marked the beginning of open season on grouse and woodcock and, for two and one-half glorious months, all other forms of sport were forgotten.

December, traitorous month, ended everything. There was nothing left for a disconsolate boy to do but saw wood and work. The one thing which kept me from pining away from sheer ennui was an occasional day spent in hunting rabbits or tending a few, scattering, fox traps. The sly little chap outclassed me for many winters but, at last, I succeeded in fooling some of the less cunning ones.

It seemed a weary while from eight to sixteen. Interminable years that dragged by with leaden feet. Ah, foolish, impatient youth, they were golden years. Halcyon years— and, too late, we awaken to find they are gone, forever.

There were incidents that enlivened the period, however, and some of them stand out sharply in my memory. The selection of my first bird dog was one of the big events of my life. I saw him first ere his soft brown eyes opened to the light of day, and vowed to move heaven and earth to make him mine. It was almost necessary to do that, for there was stern parental opposition to the plan from both sides of the house. But, as vehemently as they upheld the negative, I supported the affirmative. I implored, entreated, beseeched, supplicated, with prayer and fasting for forty days, and in the end, I think they realized I wanted a dog. When at last, Mother, in desperation, raised her hands to high heaven and said, "For goodness sake, go and get him," I was gone ere her words had ceased to echo from the kitchen walls.

Ah, Gyp, I loved you—passionately—truly. And now, after more than thirty years, I can tell you that I loved you better than I have ever since loved another of your kind. You deserved it, old boy, for you were mine, and mine alone. We knew that, you and I. Ah, faithful little Gyp, I hope your sleep is sweet.

Dad's first goose was a highlight in those days and an

incident never forgotten by the family. Dad undoubtedly would have forgotten, but he was reminded of it on suitable occasions and thus the memory was kept green.

It was in the spring of the year, and I am led to believe, on a Tuesday morning. On Monday afternoon a storm came rolling in from the sea and by night had reached hurricane proportions. During the evening Mother fretted because the family wash was on the line, from which I deduce it was Monday evening.

I remember how the house rocked and groaned from the power of that tremendous wind, and of Dad's remarking that all the ducks and geese in the world would be seeking shelter on the marshes.

We went to bed and fell asleep to the accompaniment of tortured timbers and creaking blinds, and awoke the next morning to find an early May sun shining serenely from a turquoise sky.

There was planting to be done in the field near the pasture, and after the morning chores Dad and I sallied forth to do it.

We crossed the plowed field, ankle-deep in black mud, and were nearing the pasture when Dad suddenly dropped to his knees and pulled me down beside him.

"Goose!" he whispered, excitedly. "There's a goose in that clump of alders in the pasture." He pointed with nervous forefinger, and I saw it instantly. A magnificent goose, half as large as a sheep, standing in the very edge of a patch of low alders some hundred or more yards away.

He had not seen us yet, we judged, for he remained stationary, only occasionally twisting his body about, and ever and anon lifting one wing partly out from his body and stretching it stiffly.

"He's been hurt in the storm," said Dad. "You stay here and watch him, and I'll go for the gun." He pushed me flat, and turning, hurried on hands and knees toward the house.

I watched the goose, with mouth watering as I visualized him roasting in our oven. I had seen plenty of geese before, but never one like this fellow. Grandfather of them all he was, and I waited with pounding heart for Dad and the 10 gauge. He came presently, creeping, puffingly, up behind me and pushing that monstrosity of a gun before him. He passed me, eyes fastened on that majestic bird, and I wriggled along behind him in the path he made. Twenty yards ahead was a shallow ditch that ran quarteringly past our quarry. If we could make that without frightening him, we could follow it until we were within range. We made it, cautiously, and with a sigh of relief dropped down into it— and into four inches of water. The ditch was too shallow to afford cover in any way but one, and that way was still on hands and knees. Dad went to it, as eager as a bird dog drawing scent, and I followed closely as a spaniel at heel.

Since then I have crawled, flat on my tummy, through mud and slime, to come within range of geese on the marshes, but the way never seemed so long again. We made it after interminable minutes, and Dad pushed the gun over the bank and cautiously lifted his head. I lifted mine likewise, just as Old Betsy vomited fire and lead. The young alder leaves flew in a cloud, and the goose shook violently but remained upright. Instantly the other barrel roared, and that majestic bird shuddered spasmodically as the charge struck home, but refused to lose his footing.

"I brought only two shells," Dad muttered. "He must be badly hurt; perhaps we can catch him." He dropped the gun on the grass, sprang to his feet and dashed away, and as fast as I could, I followed him.

Forty yards away the goose calmly watched our headlong approach. Thirty-five yards, thirty, twenty-five—and Dad came to a sudden halt, and as I came pounding up, turned to me. For the first and last time in my life I saw him ashamed of something he had done.

"What is it, Dad?"

Without answering he led the way up to that lordly bird, and then I saw.

There was a baby in the house, and some of the apparel

so peculiarly necessary to babies of whatever persuasion was hanging on the line during the storm. Coming loose in the night it had blown across the fields, pausing on that soggy plowed ground long enough to take on coloring matter so artistically that a nature artist, seeing it, would have turned a shamrock hue with envy; and then, tempest-borne, draped itself about a young alder, where it swayed convincingly in each vagrant breeze.

We took it to the house, and Mother, a sensible woman and one not given to an overly display of emotion, laughed until she had hysterics. If, at rare intervals in the years that followed, Dad ever hinted that some bit of management on her part might, by a disinterested party, be technically termed a mistake, it was only necessary for her to ask, "Charles, do you remember the time you shot the goose?" whereupon the matter would be laid on the table.

I remember, too, that I engaged briefly in the banking business in those years. For some time I had entertained the desecrating thought that the 10 gauge was a trifle too heavy for my youthful physique and had set my heart on a little Belgian 12 gauge that, magnetically, drew me to the store window where it was displayed.

Dad loyally consented to its purchase on the condition I save one-half of the fifteen dollars it cost, hence my activities in the realms of high finance.

Pennies and dimes went into the bank zealously and, in the evenings, I gloated over them like a miser over his gold. New and mysterious ways were opened for me to find lucrative employment—ways for which I now believe Dad was responsible—and the fund grew nobly.

I might have become a third Rockefeller or Morgan had I not been so indiscreet as to take up science in a big way. I became suddenly and intensely interested in some phases of the manufacture of glass. For a laboratory I had an unused greenhouse on a neighboring farm. My scientific instruments consisted of an air rifle and a handful of BB shot. The problem involved was why, at the impact of a leaden pellet, one square of glass would shatter beautifully, a second would radiate myriad fine lines from a common center, while the third stood the test with admirable fortitude.

How high the youthful Edison would have climbed is problematical, for an irate owner discovered my presence. I was evicted, like Adam from the Garden, and the matter was laid, although not by me, before the man higher up. Judgment was in favor of the plaintiff. The verdict against the defendant was as follows, namely and to wit: a full and complete restoration of all fractured material, said restoration being backed to the limit of the resources of the First Bank of America. There was but one alternative and that was a trip to the woodshed with Dad. That loomed, in my imagination, with all the terrors of the Black Hole of Calcutta so, with heavy heart, I chose the lesser of the two evils.

Those were drab days. The putty was flintlike in its hardness, my fingers were cut in scores of places and my hands were blistered and raw. I knew, however, that my punishment was a just one and, in the weary hours, my laggard brain had ample time to reason the thing out. Since then I have rigorously schooled myself to respect the property of others and have found it pays big dividends, aside from the morals involved.

There are numerous posted covers, in my hunting territory, where I can park my car in the owner's dooryard, chat a few minutes with the folks, hunt as long as I choose and come back to find the lady of the house waiting for me, with a plate of cookies in one hand and a glass of milk in the other. No personal charm of mine is responsible. They believe me to be reasonably honest and know I will respect the privilege they have granted me. I like them, genuinely for their own worth, and they give me their friendship in return.

The end of my activities as a glazier also marked the closing, forever, of the bank of which I was president and in which I had been the heaviest depositor. That was a dark period through which no ray of light shone. The summer, with its numerous opportunities for raising pennies, had passed and the bird hunting season was close at hand. I sincerely believed I could not exist without that gun and yet I saw no possible chance of acquiring it. For days I sat, a replica of Rodin's Thinker, but found no solution to my problem.

Worried, pale and distraught, I was in no condition to withstand the next wallop from Old Man Fate and it floored me completely. Someone had bought the little gun and the storekeeper was strangely unable to remember the person's name.

"Dunno's he told me what his name was," he said. "I don't ricollect askin' him, either. Kind of a medium-sized feller he was. Taller'n a short man an' shorter'n a tall one. Had some hair on his head, seems if. I don't remember very good."

Visions of finding the new owner and offering him a bonus, verbally, faded. Through my own foolishness I had thrown away the thing I most prized and now I was paying the penalty to the last, full measure.

Then, one glorious morning, my waking eyes beheld it lying on a chair by my bedside. No gift from the gods, this. No necromancy or legerdemain. Dad's kindly hands had placed it there.

I have owned better guns since then. In fact, now that I

pause to consider the matter, I believe it, without question, to have been the worst specimen of the gunsmith's art ever to come out of Belgium. It disintegrated, like the "Wonderful One Hoss Shay," ere I had owned it a year. It may be that I wore it out with too much cleaning, for no weapon was ever polished more meticulously or often. The wonderful Damascus finish disappeared completely, I remember, ere the hunting season opened and with every discharge of the piece something rattled off or flew from it. I was mechanically inclined and kept it functioning for almost a year when, metaphorically, it threw up its hands and quit. I was not totally unprepared, however. For months I had watched over it, like a mother over an ailing infant, and the shock of its demise, although severe, was not paralyzing.

I was not wholly without funds and was possessed of certain bits of personal property which had some intrinsic worth. By a carefully worked out system of barter, from which I believe I received not less than fifty cents on the dollar, I acquired an American-made hammerless which was a thing of beauty and a joy for—not forever, but for some months, at least. It was a double gun in every sense of the word. I had not owned it a week when it developed the unpleasant trait of occasionally releasing the second hammer at the recoil of the first discharge, and no amount of filing the sears would effect a permanent cure.

It did that morale-lowering trick scores of times on single birds but, so perverse was its nature, not once, in the two years I owned it, did it ever do so when there was a possible chance of making a double. Had it not been for the thorough rough-housing Old Betsy had given me I am sure I would have developed an incurable case of flinching, for I know of no more nerve-trying ordeal than that of anticipating a recoil which fails to come until momentarily forgotten.

In addition to these peculiarities, that abomination was the only one I ever saw which would "ball" a charge of shot. I have heard of it frequently, in fact, it used to be a time-honored alibi for missing an easy shot. But this gun, to my certain knowledge, did it several times. One grouse gave me an open cross-shot at forty yards. The charge centered her perfectly and opened not larger than a silver dollar. I might state, in passing, it was a clean, no, a decidedly unclean kill.

A black duck, flying overhead at about the same distance, was decapitated as cleanly as a chicken beneath the axe. A woodcock vanished utterly, in thin air, and left only a faint halo of feathers around the spot he had occupied a split second before.

These, and sundry other defections, cooled my ardor and we were divorced the following autumn.

Then came a period of barter and exchange which lifted me from the novice class and made me, in a few years, almost a professional.

The knowledge of gun value becomes instinctive after a time and is almost uncanny in its accuracy. The lines and finish of a good gun may be copied faithfully in a cheap imitation, but one possessed with that intuitive feeling toward craftsmanship will glance, casually, at a dealer's rack, in which a score of guns are displayed, and unerringly pick out the two or three which possess genuine quality.

I learned much in those days, most of which I have long since forgotten, and drew one definite conclusion to which I still firmly adhere. Not only in the end but, from the beginning, quality pays.

I suppose, on looking back, I must have been an energetic youth, for I accumulated money from various sources —honestly, for the greater part and, for the remainder, as honestly as is consistent with gun trading. But, from whatever devious ways the money came, it was all diverted into one well worn channel. I bought ammunition, by the case, by the thousand, in orders second only to that of the United States Army. I bought bullet moulds for dozens of rifles and powder by the keg. The old farmhouse and the surrounding outbuildings were a well stocked armory. I remember that I developed the habit of holding my breath

during severe thunderstorms, not through fear of the lightning bolt but in the uncertain conjecture as to how high we
would go if those stored explosives ignited simultaneously.

In after years, certain persons have insinuated that I was
born a good shot but such is far from being a fact. No boy
ever worked harder than I to acquire the tools of the trade
and none practiced more assiduously.

"Count that day lost whose low, descending sun
  Is not, in part, obscured by powder from my gun,"

was my motto, and I lived up to it faithfully. With a 22 I
shot at objects thrown in the air; I shot at blocks swinging
on a string, at revolving targets; at targets suspended from
an oval-shaped wheel which in turn ran down an inclined
wire. I shot at stationary objects—from shoulder and hip,
with one eye shut, with both eyes open. With the aid of a
mirror I shot at objects behind me.

As much as I could afford, I used a shotgun in the same
manner, and each day I practiced throwing it to my shoulder, with head erect, and then lowering my eyes to ascertain
how nearly it pointed to some previously selected mark.

This was madness, I know, but there was method in it.
Speed and accuracy were the elusive qualities I was trying
to capture, and I had as little of both as anyone in the world.
I was a grouse hunter by this time and had come to know

that I would always be one. I had hunted some with the best wing shot our community ever knew. He outclassed me so far that I knew I could never approach his effortless ease, his uncanny accuracy, but I knew that, with what will power I had, I would try and try and keep on trying.

It was a discouraging time. After a whole summer of practice on inanimate objects I would enter the woods in the fall with all the confidence of the Duke of Wellington. I would, I assured myself, make of each cover a downy bed of grouse feathers. I would reduce the grouse population to the point of extinction. Men would nudge their companions and whisper as I passed, "That fellow is the best pa'tridge shot in the United States."

Then, day after day, I would miss everything that fluttered a wing. Straightaway, quartering, or cross-shots, it made no difference; I missed them all.

Literally I shot at hundreds of grouse each season for several years before I could average to kill one bird with each twenty-five shells, and if that isn't disgraceful enough to console the heart of any tyro, I'll rewrite this paragraph and, still telling the truth, give him better odds.

I must have been about twenty years of age when I discovered my fault. For years I had practiced for speed—and more speed—and it was an essential thing. To locate the sound of wings instantly, to swing the gun in the direction of the sound and to the shoulder, simultaneously, is a necessity, but the actual squeezing of the trigger must be, for me at least, a rather leisurely affair. When I learned that fact and had practiced it conscientiously for a year or two, I knew at last the joy that must have been that of my old friend Carney when he said, "What! Me swap places with Rockefeller? Hell! I can kill more birds than he can."

CHAPTER III

MY intimate association with grouse has extended over a period of nearly forty years. In that time I have come to regard him as the wisest and, also, the most foolish of birds. His keenness of sight and hearing is a thing to marvel at. His knowledge as to the psychological moment for bursting into sudden, startled and startling flight is a thing which he has acquired from countless ancestors.

Through what process of instinct or reason this glorious bird has come to realize that only through invisibility, even while on the wing, is he safe, is a thing to ponder over. He knows it, however, and he knows it thoroughly. Hundreds of times I have caught grouse in positions where they had to fly a number of feet to gain cover. That cover might be the bole of a single big tree, or perhaps an evergreen but a few feet high. It has been a delight to see the bird explode (that word seems to best describe the action) into instantaneous, full speed in the direction of that bit of protecting cover. Oftentimes, to reach it, he must fly nearer to me than when he started.

Many times he comes so near that I, involuntarily, dodge to give him room to pass. His bright, shoe-button eye peers up at me as he hurtles past and he whistles a soft little "quit—quit—quit." A split second before he reaches that bit of cover he banks sharply, with a tilt of his wide-spreading tail, and slides in behind that sheltering screen. As he disappears from view his head is still turned. One beady eye watches me while the other charts the course ahead as he glides, swiftly out of gunshot.

He will sit as immovable as a stone while you tramp past him within a score of feet. Then, when you have stepped behind a bush, he will hammer out behind you, causing you to turn completely about to locate him, a physical contortion which is not conducive of steady shooting.

He will perch on the branch of a tree and peer down at you while you pretend not to see him and tramp, sturdily, past until you have reached that spot you have in mind where it will be necessary for him to give you a fairly open shot.

Then, when you slip the safety off the gun, and turning, say, "All right, old fellow. Do your stuff," he perversely refuses to fly. After a moment you look down for a stick or stone to toss at him, and—"Whirr-r-r!" he is gone —over your head, directly back through the tree, or hardest of all, in a rushing sweep down to within a few inches of the ground. When you can stop them in the midst of that maneuver, you are privileged to tip your hat to the image that confronts you in the mirror.

He will run ahead of your dog from one bit of protecting cover to the next, for hundreds of yards, until he tires of the game, whereupon he will run through a tangle of thick foliage and flush instantly when he reaches the clearing beyond.

I remember one wise old cock who fooled me for several years so nicely, so smoothly, and so consistently that the hunting of him became a sort of rite with me; a rite which I religiously performed several times each fall, until, through no fault of mine, we drifted apart. During those years I learned, firstly, to respect him for his superior woodsmanship and then, later, to like him for himself alone. The last two years my affection for the old fellow was genuine, and although I tried every trick I knew to get one close, open shot at him during that period, I vowed that, should I ever do so, I would not pull the trigger.

He was distrustful of me, and rightly so, for I treated him shamefully on our first meeting. It was my first trip to a glorious cover so remote and inaccessible that only a few of the incurables hunt it. The very beginning of this bit of Paradise, a remote mountain valley, is a spot favored particularly by woodcock. Singularly, for such is not usually the case, it is also very fine grouse cover.

On that day, I had just entered the woods when the dog came to a staunch point. By his bulging eyes I judged the bird was close by, so I stepped directly in front of him. A woodcock arose almost at my feet and bounced up toward the tree tops. It was an easy shot, and I killed her, broke the gun, tossed away the empty shell, and was reaching for a fresh one when a magnificent cock grouse hammered up through the trees before me.

That is always an awkward position to be in when a bird flushes. Part of a precious second is lost in trying to decide which is the quicker, to thrust the fresh shell into the empty chamber or to drop it back in the pocket, close the gun and shoot the other barrel. I chose the latter course, snapped the gun to my shoulder, and shot, but I knew, while pulling the trigger, I was too slow. He had gained his coveted shelter ere the shot splashed in behind him, but he had not come through unscathed, for there were a few bits of feathers in the air where he had been a split second before. We followed, but the dog failed to locate him. He had changed his course or had treed so that we missed him, and I saw him no more that fall. The next year there was a tremendously big cock in that bit of woods. He was an old bird and a wary one, and I had a feeling it was the same grouse I had shot at the previous fall. He had matriculated in the school of experience, and made the dog and me look foolish.

There was a flock of young birds there, too, and they were unusually shy for such a remote covert. I visited the place several times that season and found the old fellow waiting for me each time. The moment the dog winded him that old cock would start running, along a hardwood ridge, down through a little valley, up a bank, and through a patch of pines. He would travel fast, and the moment he came to the clearing beyond the pine growth he would take wing. I could hear the thunder of his take-off while I was still fifty yards away.

Beyond thinking that here was a particularly shy old grouse, I gave the matter no serious consideration until the same thing had happened several times. Then it gradually dawned on me that here was a bird who was having a quiet laugh at my expense, and I decided to match my wits against his.

Accordingly I took a boy with me, and when we reached the covert, put the dog on leash and gave the youth orders to release and follow the dog in ten minutes. Then, by a roundabout course I made my way to the clearing beyond the pines where the old fellow took to the air, took my stand on a big stump just back of the stone wall that marked the boundary of that bit of pine growth, and waited to see what would happen. In a few minutes I heard the tinkle of the bell on the dog and the crashing of brush under the hurrying feet of the boy. A moment later my very shy friend hopped on the stone wall some twenty yards before me. He spotted me instantly, and his head bobbed inquisitively as he looked me over.

"Come on," I invited. "See if you can make it across the clearing this time," whereupon he turned, dropped back on the further side of the wall, ran thirty yards back in the pines, almost directly toward the dog, and rocketed up through the trees and away for hundreds of yards up the steep mountain-side where I would not follow.

Several times each year for two years more I tried every trick I knew to outwit that wily old general. I entered the woods from every side, but never once was I able to drive him into a corner. Several times I saw him running where I could have killed him, but never again, after that first time, did he make the mistake of getting into the air within forty yards of me.

Another thing I noticed, as time went on, was the increasing wariness of the other grouse in that section. It had always been a keen delight to hunt that covert, for the birds were so little molested that they would lie like woodcock, but with each passing year they became more difficult to work, running like turkeys at the first alarm. Whether they had learned this from association with that wise old drummer, or whether his caution and cunning had been bred into the younger birds, I do not know.

When, in the fifth consecutive shooting season, I failed

to start the old fellow, I felt a keen personal loss. I had grown to like him, and I am sure I would not have killed him then, had the chance occurred; but he had gone forever. I do not believe any other hunter killed him fairly. He may have been ambushed and slain, but I prefer to think otherwise. Far better the silent swoop of a giant owl in the blackness of a stormy night, or the ice sheet forming over the deep snows which were his winter bed, freezing overhead, drop by drop, as they formed that glistening white pall from which there is no escape—the glistening white pall of death.

I go back there once each year, but the woods seem somber and cheerless. The north wind sucks down through that giant pass in the hills and chills the marrow in my bones. The warmth and friendliness of the place are gone, and the hills seem steeper than in those other days. Can it be that I am growing old, or do I miss the gay, bold spirit which made of self-confident, conceited me, and clever, bird-wise old Duke, a pair of the rankest of rank amateurs?

The wisdom of the ruffed grouse is unquestioned; yet it is always a source of wonder to me why he, with his college education, will do the many fool things he is guilty of.

He will sit in the road, apparently unmindful of the approach of your car, nor will the squealing of your brakes, as you jam them on to avoid running him down, frighten him unduly. If you are so minded you may stop your car, step out with the gun in your hand, load it, and murder him in cold blood. The chances are about three to five in your favor if you care for that sort of slaughter.

Thousands of otherwise rational grouse commit suicide in that manner each fall, and far too many men make a practice of driving over the country roads with a shotgun across their laps, during the open season.

A grouse will fly through trees and brush at full speed a hundred times, and never ruffle a feather; yet if you drive that same bird across an opening which contains a house or barn, it is not at all unusual for him to crash into it with all the reckless abandon of a drunken truck-driver attacking a railway train.

He will run ahead of your dog and flush out of range a half dozen times. Then at the next point he may sit beneath a bush, which he well knows is absolutely no protection, and insist on your kicking him before he will fly.

On rare occasions he will come into your hen-yard, and while there, will act as though he were one of the flock. Once, while looking at a flock of brown leghorns with the friend to whom they belonged, I heard him give a startled exclamation. "I'll be dog-goned," he said, and he pointed to a group of hens busily scratching in a pile of litter in a fence corner. "Look there, will you!"

I looked. There may have been a dozen hens in that particular group, and striding about among them, apparently unaware of our presence, was a magnificent cock grouse. With all the arrogance of a Beau Brummel he was airing his graces before those unappreciative females. We approached slowly, penning the hens in that fence corner. They showed more agitation than did the grouse and at the last, darted past us. Not so the grouse. He stood as serenely confident as Napoleon, while my friend stooped over and gathered him in his hands.

We examined him carefully. He seemed to be uninjured, so we took him outside the fence and placed him on the sward. He looked about, turned, and took a few hesitating steps toward the hens behind us, then paused and looked up at us. He seemed to be seeing us for the first time, and I saw that look of the untamed come into his beady eyes. Instantly he turned from us and took one or two slow steps, while the blue-black ruff stood straight out on his neck. Then, a creature of the wild again, he ran a few quick steps and burst into that exquisite, startled flight which no other bird can equal.

A grouse is extremely cautious and always apprehensive of danger, but as a rule he seems to have no preconceived plan of action. The relative position of his enemy and himself when his one-track mind prompts him to take flight,

[33]

seems to be the factor which determines his line of flight. I remember one occasion when my shooting companion and I drove a flock of several grouse the length of a covert some five hundred yards long and nearly as wide. They were wild, and flushed ahead of the dog beyond shooting range. Straight ahead they went, all rising at once, and we followed, knowing their last flight would carry them to the edge of the wood. Beyond lay an open field, and it seemed quite certain they would lie well to the dog ere they broke across the clearing or back over our heads.

The dog worked ahead and pointed where we knew quite well the birds would be, and we grinned knowingly at each other, pulled our sleeves up to the wrists and worked in, prepared for a few glorious moments of intense action.

Again they went up, well out of gunshot, and across the open field. A hundred yards out in that field was a little depression some fifty feet across, and in it grew a matted tangle of high-bushed blueberries. There was no other cover near, and we knew that no grouse with a modicum of brains would stop in a place like that—but every last bird dropped into that little patch of bushes and stayed there.

Now here, we told ourselves, was a chance such as seldom came to grouse hunters. We would separate, and come down on them in such a manner that no matter which way they went, one of us would be within range.

We did that, making a wide detour, and came down on that little patch of bushes from opposite sides. We were within range now, thirty yards—twenty—ten. The dog was pointing staunchly on the windward side. We had made no mistake, the grouse was there—but why didn't they get up? We advanced the few remaining steps to the edge of the bushes, and still not a bird moved.

I kicked a bush, and instantly we could hear them whistling that soft little "quit-quit-quit" of alarm.

"Look out for the low ones," said my companion, from the other side of the bushes, which were a little more than waist-high. An ambiguous phrase, that,—the argot of a bird hunter. Translated, it means the speaker has no irresistible longing to have a few hundred shot extracted from his quivering flesh.

"Watch out! I'm going to throw a rock in there."

"O.K. Let 'er go."

Crash! Thr-r-r-up! A lone grouse hammered up head-high, spotted us instantly, and dropped into the brush.

"They're over on this side now. Watch out. I'll throw this stick in there."

Whish-sh! Thr-r-r-r-up! Exactly the same as before, another grouse got up to the top of the bushes and dropped instantly back.

"Send the dog in and let him put them up."

[35]

"Send him in yourself—if you think you can. He'll point there until we are gray headed if the birds lie. He's staunch, that dog."

"Great chance for a double, or a pair of them, if we can only get them up."

"I've hunted pa'tridge for twenty years and I'll be damned if I ever saw anything like this. Five minutes ago they were as wild as a bunch of chorus girls, and now you couldn't make 'em fly with a charge of dynamite."

"Let's work in a little way together, and don't shoot at singles. That would be too easy. Let's see if a pair will get up together."

"All right, let's go."

We took a few cautious steps into the brush and "Whir-r-r—Whir-r-r;" a pair got up simultaneously and started for the woods. I swung on the left hand bird and pulled the trigger. "Crack!" Both birds collapsed and dropped dead in the open field.

"Hey! Did you shoot?"

"Of course I shot. Do you think I'm paralyzed or something?"

"Well, you spoiled my double."

"Your double? All right. We're even, then, for you spoiled mine."

We backed out, cautiously, and gathered up the birds.

The dog was still frozen, motionless, on point. We looked at him, and then at each other.

"What do you say?" I asked. "Shall we try it again?"

"Hell, no," he said, in the mild, expressionless manner which is his custom. "That's premeditated murder. Let 'em live."

We left them there, but we went back again, a week later. That day was one of the many I shall never forget. More birds had come into the covert and they lay perfectly for the dog. We were in top form, that day, and took the limit with hardly a miss, and departed with the comfortable assurance that there were more than enough birds remaining for breeders the next year.

CHAPTER IV

DESPITE the fact that, until late in the season, they are not heavily feathered, a grouse is an extremely hard bird to kill outright.

There was a time when I believed otherwise and argued that one heavy shot through the body of a grouse meant sure death. It does—but the chances are about fifty-fifty that the bird will never go into your game pocket, but will die in the woods.

I have heard many a deer hunter say that his favorite quarry possessed more energy and could carry off more lead than any other American game, figuring on a pound for pound basis.

I have killed a few deer but have never had but one drop in his tracks. He was shot through the spine. Some of the others were heart shots (in two instances that organ was blown to bits) yet they ran fast and far.

Superficially, this would seem to strengthen the argument advanced by my deer hunting friends but, on closer analysis, it becomes weakened.

Those two bucks I mentioned received one shot each from a 303. Let us suppose I had been armed with a super gun, capable of releasing several hundred of these bullets at the same time. Suppose twenty-five, or more, of these had

[39]

found their mark. Would that animal have traveled a hundred or more yards? I think not.

But, on a pound for pound ratio, many a grouse flies away with that load and, without a good dog—and oftentimes with one—is lost forever.

As unbelievable as it may sound, I have seen a grouse, half decapitated by that selfsame 303, with its skull cavity entirely emptied of its abundant supply of gray matter, fly as straight and true as an arrow. I have no doubt he would, by this time, be making his thirteenth lap around the world had he not crashed, head on, into an old timber pine some forty yards away. That, of course, was muscular reaction over which he had no control but, try the same thing on your next deer and see what happens.

I have seen scores of hard hit grouse, and by that I mean birds with several shot through the body, fly on and on until it seemed they would never stop. Some, I am led to believe, never did. I recall the incident of one bird that gave me a perfect cross-shot in a clearing some two hundred yards across. When I squeezed the trigger I knew, for a certainty, that bird was mine. He had ceased his tremendous, driving wing motion in that instant and had started the long and deceivingly fast glide which would carry him across the clearing to the rock-strewn, wooded bank he had chosen for his haven.

The shot struck home, heavily, for he was very near. I looked for him to collapse but, instead, his wings again took up that vibrating drive. That he was a dead bird I knew, therefore I did not shoot again but watched him closely.

As straight and true as an arrow, never deviating a hair's breadth from his course, he flew the remaining distance across the clearing to the rock-strewn bank and crashed, head on, into an immense boulder on the hillside.

In my younger days I once centered a grouse that was coming back over my head. I was shooting an automatic 12 gauge at the time, and there were five shells in it when I started operations. As the shot hit him he abruptly ceased his forward progress and centered every energy on the task of keeping afloat. Later in life I would have dropped the gun, seized my trusty notebook, and accurately recorded the subsequent happenings; but at that time I had the impetuosity of youth, and so continued lining him up and pulling the trigger. I emptied the gun, walking slowly to keep under him, for he had a slight drift to the leeward.

Each shot denuded him further of feathers, but the more he lost and the more ballast he accumulated, the faster those wings beat. At last, with empty gun, I watched him, too fascinated to think of reloading. He still drifted slowly down wind and, without hurrying, I walked beneath him.

How far I would have walked I do not know but, fortunately, at that moment Sir Isaac Newton discovered the law of gravity and my bird, together with several ounces of lead, came down with a dull and sickening thud.

On five different occasions I have observed the unusual phenomenon of a "towering" bird. In each instance where I secured the specimen, I found only one shotmark in the skin, and that just back of the eye.

My theory of the singular performance is that the shot has only sufficient energy to penetrate to the optic nerve or nerves, where it lodges. The paralyzed nerve causes temporary blindness, but otherwise the bird is physically fit for minutes of intense action. It cannot see to make a landing, and every instinct tells it to keep flying; consequently it tips instantly and sharply upward, and begins a spiral flight straight for high heaven.

Usually, if the wind is not strong enough to cause a drift, the flight is practically vertical. Altitude is gained slowly, and at such tremendous effort that it hastens the end. Abruptly the wings cease to beat, and the bird is dead in mid-air. I have seen the flight continue for several minutes, although in my experience, I doubt if the ultimate height has ever exceeded two hundred yards.

A grouse-hunting friend, whose veracity I accept without question, told me that, on an overcast day with a fine drizzle of rain in the air, he had the novel experience of seeing one "tower" until it was lost to his view. There was no wind, and he waited long, but the bird failed to drop back to earth. Undoubtedly he did, ultimately, for everything that goes up must come down.

The question which naturally arises in the mind of the novice is: "How then may I kill grouse cleanly and reduce the large proportion of 'feathered' birds which get away?"

My experience has been that with fine shot I have less cripples. For a number of years I shot 10s wholly until the leaves were well off the trees; then I changed to 9s; and at the very last of the season, in open shooting, I used 7½s.

Now I use 9s the season through, in a cylinder bore, and rigorously school myself to shoot at no bird over thirty-five yards away. If I center my bird at that distance, it is an unusual occurrence when he does not fall.

It is logical to suppose that the larger the number of shot in a charge, the greater the chance of breaking a bone, and any broken bone, other than one in the leg, is a very serious handicap to anything navigating the air. If I have a good retrieving dog, I would rather have a bird drop with only one broken wing than to have her fly fifty yards and drop dead. My dog's chances of finding her are infinitely greater.

It is surprising what little force is necessary to snap the

wing-bone of a grouse in rising flight. Evidently they are subjected to nearly a breaking strain, for I have seen them shatter unbelievably at the impact of only one shot.

How a grouse, flying at the tremendous speed they attain, can be thus crippled and fall through trees and brush, only to strike the ground right side up and otherwise uninjured, has always been a mystery to me. But they can do it. I do not, at the moment, recall having ever seen a broken-winged bird killed by that crash, which is to me, and must be to him also, a soul-stirring one.

It has been my practice for years to go in quickly when I know my bird is a wing-broken one. He knows a moment or two of indecision after his sudden contact with Mother Earth, and in those few moments I plan to get within sight of him. The dog would undoubtedly find him, but it saves time. Also, I occasionally get an added thrill when, in the midst of that sudden dash, another bird goes up. That is a test of speed and accuracy. If you can come to a plunging halt, off balance, and swing on him when he has little more than a score of feet to go to reach cover, hurrying as fast as you can, and then take the last hundredth of a second which can possibly be spared, to assure yourself you are holding true, you're there, my son!

The art of distinguishing between a wing-broken and a body-hit bird is not a difficult one to learn. The bird killed

[44]

in mid-air falls headlong, oftentimes with wings folded, in a more or less graceful curve.

The wing-broken one falls jerkily, sidewise, its one good wing often turning him over in mid-air. If only the wing tip is broken, he comes down in a long, sweeping curve, runs when he hits the earth, and is usually a hard bird to find.

How marvelous a thing is memory! My pen formed the words "wing tip," and immediately I recalled an incident which happened when I was a youngster. I remember it for several reasons. It was the first time in my life I ever bagged four grouse in one day. It was the first time I had ever beaten —but that's the story.

For several years, when it could be arranged—the arranging, by the way, being all on my part—I hunted with Dave Harmon. He was tall and thin, and moved on a sidewalk as though he feared something was due to break at any moment; but in the brush with a shotgun in his hands, he was the smoothest, full-floating, quiet roller-bearing machine it had ever been my lot to see in operation. It was a marvel to me to see him kill grouse, and, after the years, I still believe he was just about as good as they come.

It was said of him that no matter how many grouse his companion might take in any one day, he would bag as many or more.

My experience with him was that he would manage to give me four-fifths of the shots, and then trim me unmercifully; but one day—

We were hunting a remarkably good covert that afternoon, and the birds were all breaking in my direction. I was plentifully supplied with ammunition and succeeded in bagging two grouse by mid-afternoon. Then, in getting around the dog, who was on point, I blundered on a pair of birds. They made their one great mistake when they chose to fly past Dave, for he took them both with a clean, snappy double.

For another hour I did what shooting was done, and as a result of that wild fusillade, added one more grouse to my collection.

Did I feel happy? I did. I had tied my former high record of three and had the champion one up.

Then, as the sun was going down, he got his third shot for the day, and we were all even again.

To be tied with that superman was something that had never happened to me before. I liked the sensation and felt that it would be nice to go home—for once—in that happy state of mind.

Accordingly I suggested that, as the walk was long, we had better start for home. He readily agreed, and we started off. We had almost reached the road, which marked the end of our hunting and the beginning of the long tramp home, when a pair of grouse flushed far ahead and to our right. Dusk was falling, and they were out of gunshot when they started, but one of them rocketed up to the top of the trees and quartered back against the sky line at an angle which brought him past me at a distance of perhaps sixty yards.

In those youthful days, if a grouse was within range of my vision, I saluted him with at least one barrel. I knew this bird to be too far away, but instinct brought the gun to my shoulder. I held well in advance and pulled the trigger.

"Too far!" said my companion, and in that instant the grouse tipped slightly downward and began a long curving descent.

"Wing-tipped," he said instantly. "Let's get after her fast. The dog will find her."

We went on the run, and a hundred yards away the dog picked up scent and started trailing. We followed closely, tripping over brush and vines, for the twilight was deepening rapidly. Fifty yards further on, the dog came to a point beside a large brush-pile. We peered in, trying to locate the bird, but could see nothing of her.

There was but one thing to do and we did it. We moved that pile of brush to the last, tangled limb, the dog still pointing staunchly, and no sign of the grouse anywhere.

Under the brush-pile was an old stump with wide-spreading roots. We got down on our hands and knees and groped in the hollows beneath them, and at last there came a welcome flutter and *I had my fourth grouse.*

There was a faint rosy light in the western sky. The sun had gone—irrevocably and too soon—but a crescent moon was there to see, and the stars came shyly, one by one, to peep down on the prodigy of the century.

Nonchalantly I stuffed the bird in my bulging coat, trying to conceal my elation, while one thought kept hammering in my brain until I longed to hop upon a fallen tree, beat my manly breast like a braggart rooster, and shout that all the world might hear: "I have beaten him—I have beaten him."

There was no chance for him now to stage a last-minute recovery, for night was only a matter of minutes away.

So engrossed was I with the thought, that I failed to notice, for some moments, that he was gone. The sound of his footfalls in the distance brought me to myself, and I called to him.

"The road is out this way."

"I'll be right out," he answered.

Through the gathering darkness I picked my way out to the country road and paused to listen. In the distance I could hear the faint crackle of brush under his hurrying feet.

Then I heard a grouse fly, and my heart leaped to my throat, but there came no sound of the shot I had feared, my heart slid slowly back into position, and I breathed more easily. No need to worry, for it was too dark for any man to see to shoot.

His footsteps came nearer. He was accepting the inevitable and coming out of the woods, a beaten man.

Ah, well! Such was life. One could be champion only about so long, and then he met a better man.

Again a grouse flushed—nearer this time—and I heard a muttered exclamation. The words were not intelligible, but I had a feeling that had they been, I would have known exactly what they meant.

On he came, nearer each moment, until I could distinguish even the patter of the dog's feet. They stopped suddenly; brush crackled as my friend came in—and "Whir-r-r-r!" "Bang!"

Something plumped, clod like, upon the ground, and in the heavy night air a voice said distinctly, "There, damn you—now see if you can fly."

He came out a minute later with the bird in his hand. "Had to chase him all over Robin Hood's barn to get him against the sky line," was his only comment. "Well, let's go home."

No longer was I mounted on a winged Pegasus, riding

the far-flung clouds of achievement. No, I was a disillusioned youth once more, miles from home—and the way
seemed weary and long.

CHAPTER V

I HAVE shot over an old fashioned, black coated shepherd dog. Shot grouse over him, too. That's funny, isn't it? But, before your risibility becomes uncontrollable, let me tell you that his work compared favorably with that of some of the best dogs I have known.

My personal opinion is that, if a dog has a good nose, his next and most essential requirement is brains. Old Shep had all of the latter commodity his wise old head would hold.

He was trained by a man who was an exceptionally good wing shot and he had seen hundreds of grouse fall to his master's gun. They understood and loved each other, as some, fortunate, men and dogs do.

He was old when I first hunted over him but he was very wise. Here is a thing I have seen him do, not once, but many times. I will try to tell it accurately, without elaboration, describing his actions as I remember them, and let you be the judge of his bird sense.

On many occasions, when I chanced to be nearer to him than was his master, I have seen him come out of the brush and plant himself directly in my path, looking up at me eagerly, and emitting a soft little whine. He had an odd habit, at such times, of giving his head a slight upward and sidewise jerk, much like the unconscious gesture of a man indicating something over his shoulder. He had the most deliberately slow and convincing wink I have seen since I lost my interest in co-eds which, in combination with that intriguing gesture of the head, said so plainly that even I could understand, "Come on over here. There's something I wish to show you."

The moment he knew that I understood him, he would start off, so slowly that I could easily walk behind him, making his way straight for some spot he had previously investigated. After a time I could sense a caution in his advance, and he would glance back at me from time to time as though to adjure me to a less noisy approach.

At last he would halt, turn about, and face me again, and if I moved aside to pass him, he would place himself directly in my path, saying unprintable things with his eyes.

Convinced at last, that my laggard brain had registered the thought that he wished me to remain stationary, he would start off at right angles to his former course, pausing once or twice to see if I was still bright enough to remain in the spot he had indicated, and then circle around in front of me, emit a short bark of warning, and come in with a rush. Invariably a grouse would rise, beating almost straight upward to elude his mad dash. They are the best of targets when they are doing that, but even so, I missed occasionally. When I did that, he came out and said things to me that even now I blush to recall.

A very noticeable thing about all his work on grouse was the lack of the deadly seriousness of the pointer or setter. Hundreds of times I have seen the protruding eyes of a solidly frozen pointer roll in their sockets to see whether or not I was ever coming up to kill that bird, and the eyes of no king whose throne was tottering ever showed half the anguish of his.

Many a setter has looked up at me with the softly pleading brown eyes that only the spaniel breed possesses, saying mutely, "Please, boss, go get him. It's a grouse, boss, a grouse."

Old Shep came out and winked at me, with a grin in his eye, and said, "What a lot of fun we're having. There's another one over here. Come on, let's go after him."

It was a game to him. He played it exceptionally well, but not too seriously—which, after all, is not a bad way to play any game.

I would not care to hunt grouse or woodcock without a dog. It can be done quite successfully on grouse—and even on woodcock at times—but for me, much of the pleasure in shooting lies in anticipating the moment when the bird will fly, and trying, with whatever woodcraft I may have learned, to outguess him. When a bird dog winds game, that anticipation becomes acute and lasts, oftentimes, for minutes before the bird is put up.

Nowhere in the animal kingdom do I know of such a remarkable instance of what careful, selective breeding can do than in the case of the pointer and setter.

The natural instinct of all the dog kind was to chase their quarry, but man, in a few hundred years, has changed what nature took eons to mould, until today, in a good setter or pointer the instinct to point is so strong that little training is necessary.

I also believe that breeding for the requirements necessary to win field trials on quail is gradually eliminating many of the qualities which are absolutely essential in a good grouse or woodcock dog.

In making this statement, I realize that I am paving the way for criticism from my many southern friends, but such is my feeling in the matter. It may be that my experience with field-trial stock has left me wrongfully prejudiced against them, but those experiences were not pleasurable ones, and in several instances were far from profitable ventures—for me.

One notable exception, however, was White Hope. He was sired by Prince Rodney's Count and was shipped north, when two years of age, for breeding purposes. I had the handling of him exclusively for three years, and he was as good and true a grouse dog as one would care to see. It was a new game to him when I first took him out, but he learned fast and what he learned he never forgot. At the last I could work him for days on end without issuing a command, and not once would he be out of control, quartering his ground thoroughly and fast without going twice over it, and keeping in touch with me all the time.

He has gone long since to other hunting grounds, but he is not forgotten. He sired many good sons and daughters while he was here, and one was the best dog over which I ever hunted.

I say that unhesitatingly, for it is true; but I say it with reluctance, for he was not mine. I have owned good dogs. I have, for short periods, owned poor ones. But never one like Count has looked up at me and said, "Hello, Boss."

He had everything a bird dog should have, and he was doubly fortunate in being blessed with a good master and having been born at a time when grouse, after several years of extreme scarcity, were coming again into a period of abundance. He was at his best for several years when there were birds everywhere, and he had more experience in each of these years than most dogs get in a lifetime.

He had the stamina to hunt day after day, growing lean and hard until he seemed to be built entirely of whalebone and rawhide. It is my firm belief that, when he reached that stage, no man lived who could hunt him off his feet. I do know that one fall we hunted him from early morn until dark each night, for five glorious weeks, with the exception of Sundays and one-half day when it rained.

We hunted in two states and we hunted fast and hard. It was our boast that we were lean and tireless ourselves but, at the last, he would leap lightly over a stone wall which we climbed slowly and unsteadily, like a couple of senile old men who had wandered afield from some Home for the Aged. He was a grouse dog par excellence, but as a woodcock dog he was, in the present-day vernacular, not so hot.

Reluctantly again, knowing I am quite likely to be court-martialed and shot at sunrise, I state that, in my experience, such has almost invariably been the case.

Strange it is, how loyal we men are to our dogs. Say to a man, "What did you ever see in that woman that caused you to wish to marry her?" and he will shake his head sadly and say, without hesitation, "Heaven only knows."

Say to him, "How did you happen to buy this car, anyway? Didn't you know that—"

"I wasn't myself, that day," he will interrupt. "Delirious or something. There ought to be a law against manufacturing a thing like that."

Say to the same man, "You have a mighty fine grouse dog here. He's one to be proud of I think, however, he takes a little too much time locating his woodcock." Say that—and see what happens.

The hair will bristle on the back of his neck, his face will turn purple and his eyes take on a baleful, reddish glare, while he proceeds to tell you things about yourself you would much prefer the world should never know.

The chances are about five to one that you are right. A good grouse dog is bold and confident, but he is very careful. He knows to an inch how far he may go in on grouse without putting them up. He will work them high headed, taking his scent from the air, and be almost infallibly accurate. Put the same dog in a covert where woodcock have been for a few days, and he will crawl about, belly to earth, sniffing the ground here and there as though uncertain where the odor was coming from. He will locate them, without error, if you give him time—but he usually needs plenty of it.

Undoubtedly there are exceptions. It may even be that my experience has been the exception and I am wrong, as usual, but I have never seen a first-class grouse dog who was equally good on woodcock, nor have I seen a dog whose work was outstanding on woodcock but had many glaring faults on ruffed grouse.

If I were buying a dog to use on grouse and woodcock, I would buy one bred from New England shooting dogs. I would insist on seeing his pedigree, that I might know he had no mongrel blood in his veins. If that pedigree showed he was several generations removed from a field-trial champion, and if he suited my fancy, I would buy him and spend the rest of my spare time making him believe I was the most wonderful person in the world.

As I write this a pair of beautiful white setters are romping just outside my window. They are picture dogs, exquisitely moulded, with heads so perfectly chiseled I am moved to exclaim with admiration. They are youngsters, up here from Alabama, to summer with a friend and neighbor of mine. They have been handled on quail in the south and have run in the Manitoba trials on chicken. For young dogs they have had considerable experience. They are valuable specimens but—

They go across an open field at a pace which would distance Man o' War in six furlongs. I have seen them come, at breakneck speed, through the brush to our river bank. Without lessening their stride by the thousandth of an inch, I have seen them plunge far out into the hurrying flood and swim as though His Satanic Majesty was only one stroke behind, then dash up the further bank and away, with all the energy and reckless abandon of a brace of straying thunderbolts.

They could be trained to hunt grouse. Twenty years

ago I would have delighted in attaching myself to the executive end of a check cord and teaching them the meaning of "Whoa." At the present time the sum total of their acquired knowledge lies in comprehending the words "Go on," and they get that only when it is wigwagged to them, from a distance of a quarter mile, by a man with a felt hat.

No. For some reason I cannot visualize myself following that pair of beauties through grouse country. I'll take one of the nasal-accented, conservative old New England stock for mine. One with a bit of Puritan blood in his veins, if you please. After I had acquired him and he had come to regard me as his deity, I would teach him a few fundamentals of grouse dog etiquette. In doing so I would always try to remember that a human being, whom we optimistically suppose to be gifted with an intelligence above the level of our four-footed friends, requires one-seventh of his lifetime to gain an average education, and I would not expect my young dog to do much better than that.

The really essential things one must teach a pup are not so numerous as some suppose. He must be gifted with a good nose and he must, sometimes, be taught staunchness. With these two, fundamental virtues he will become a valuable asset to your hunting,—if he has been blessed with a modicum of brains.

Staunchness is an often misconstrued term. It does not

mean that a dog will work in on a bird and suddenly become a bit of statuary which nothing on earth can move. It does mean that when his nose tells him he has a bird located, he should remain stationary until the bird moves on. If he is a really good dog he will then move ahead, carefully, until he has again located his quarry. If he does not do this, he lacks either experience or common sense.

Quite often the trouble lies not with the dog but with the handler. It is not unusual to see a man who should know better, hold his dog with loud and strident demands of "To-Ho," when a novice could see, by the dog's attitude and eagerness to go on, that he was no longer getting scent.

For me it is one of the most enjoyable sights in the world to watch a wise old pointer or setter trail a moving bird. Frequently a grouse will run before the hunter and his dog for hundreds of yards. I have, on rarer occasions, known them to travel a quarter mile before taking wing.

Then the dog, if he is good, follows with head held high, taking his scent entirely from the air, walking so stiff-legged that one gets the impression there are no joints in his limbs below the shoulders. Actually, he is pointing each instant but he is obliged to move to do so.

To stop a dog, under the false impression he is not staunch, when he is doing Grade A work of this type, is a crime.

A dog should retrieve. Some think it has a tendency to make him less staunch and, theoretically, this is true. If a dog sees a wounded bird on the ground and is permitted to catch it, he will have a keener desire to chase an unwounded one when he next sees it.

For that reason I would teach retrieving by the force system and would not permit him to retrieve the first season or until he had seen a goodly number of birds fall to the gun. I would always give the command "fetch" before I permitted him to go after a wounded or dead bird.

Many good dogs are not natural retrievers, and that is one of the reasons why I favor the force system of teaching it. If a dog retrieves on his own initiative only, you have no control over him, if for any reason he chooses not to do so.

Before trying to teach the system, I would familiarize myself with the method. There are several good books on the subject which are readily available. For the benefit of the novice, I will state that the system, despite its name, is a humane one and very little "force" is used.

The very best retrieving I ever saw was done by a liver-and-white pointer that I would have sacrificed much to have owned. He was trained by a different system than most, but it produced results which were a revelation to watch.

I was back hunting those glorious grouse and woodcock covers of my youth, and came, just as dusk was falling, to a crossroad and a little country store.

It had been sultry and unseasonably warm that day, and now the clouds had thickened and a thin misty rain was falling.

Approaching the store from a direction opposite to mine, came a rubber-clad hunter who, at first glance, seemed on the point of collapsing with fatigue. By his side walked a pointer, fit to adorn a bench in any dog show.

He was so physically fit, so fresh looking, that I wondered, for a moment, at his master's condition. But the wind came from his quarter and a pungent odor preceded him, an odor strangely reminiscent of the windfalls rotting beneath the apple trees on the old home farm, and I knew he had been sipping, anon, of the juice of the forbidden fruit.

He came to a shuffling halt by the store steps, seemed undecided whether to pause or not, then sat down suddenly, with startling violence, upon the lower of the three. The pointer paid no attention to my tired setter but looked at his master searchingly for a moment, then dropped at his feet.

The rubber-clad one looked me over, solemnly, through one partly opened eye.

"Hello, shranger," he said, affably. "Any luck?"

"Just a pair of grouse and three woodcock. How did they fall for you?"

"Zhore birds," he informed me, solemnly. "Pedro'n I've been hunting zhore birds. Owed it to Pedro. He ain't ever hunted zhore birds before. Thash awful shame, shranger." The tears became audible in his voice. "I used to hunt 'em year in an' year out, but Pedro nev' had a chance. Thash awful shame."

I agreed that the pity of the thing was beyond the comprehension of mortal man and asked if they found any shore birds.

"Yellow-legs," he said. "Plover all gone—curlew all gone. Jush yellow-legs lef'."

"How did the dog work on them?"

"Jush a same. Don't make any dif'rence to Old Pedro."

"He retrieves, I suppose?"

With a perceptible effort he opened the other eye and gazed up at me owlishly. Then he got shakily to his feet and began fumbling at the fastenings of his rubber coat. It opened at last, disclosing a well-worn shooting coat beneath. He slid a palsied hand in the stained pocket and drew out a moist, bedraggled yellow-leg.

"C'mon, Pedro," he suggested to the pointer. "This feller wants to know do you retrieve."

The dog got to his feet and looked up at the derelict before him. There is, hidden somewhere beneath the surface, some tremendously fine thing in any man who can draw a look like that from a dog.

For a moment they gazed thus at each other, and in the eyes of each, affection glowed.

"All right," said the stranger, and he motioned out into the gathering darkness with an unsteady hand. "Go on!"

Straight down the road the pointer went—gracefully, easily. We watched until the darkness had swallowed him, whereupon his master turned, and with what strength he could summon, threw the yellow-leg up the road.

"All right, Pedro," he called. "Come in."

The dog came back swiftly and paused before us.

"Tha's mighty tough luck," muttered the stranger. "Knocked that one down and can't find him anywhere. Yesh, sir, tha's mighty tough luck. Shertainly hate to lose that bird."

Before he was done with his halting speech the pointer was in action. He knew what was required, and he went about it in a thoroughly businesslike manner and with more system than I had seen a dog use before or have ever seen since. His first cast was a circular one of perhaps a twenty-foot radius. He did not pause to look at us as he went past but swept out in a wider arc, never hesitating, never twice covering the same ground, but out and out in ever-widening circles until he found what he sought.

He came in swiftly, joyously, and reaching up, dropped the dead bird in his master's hand.

"That's very fine work," I said, "and a mighty nice—"

"You haven't seen nothin' yet," he interrupted. "Go on out there, Pedro. I'll let you know when I want you."

Again the dog went out into the darkness, and this time two birds were thrown across the road, far out in the weeds and grass that rimmed the thoroughfare.

"Pedro."

He came in as before, and this time his master said:

" 'S a double this time. Get 'em both."

I felt this was going to be worth while; so I laid my gun on the steps, left my setter to watch it, and edged over to the grass where I could see through the darkness and rain.

The dog made three complete circles ere he winded the first bird. He came in to it as straight as a homing pigeon flies, picked it up, and turned half about, then paused and lifted his head high as he tested the heavy night air. Then he turned back, went a few steps ahead, swung sharply to the left, and went straight to the second bird.

I could not see his every movement, but I had the impression he was nosing the bird over on the ground. Just how he did it I do not know, but a moment later he dashed past me and both birds were in his mouth.

[65]

I came in to express my appreciation of this bit of work, but the stranger would not listen.

Again he motioned the dog down the road, and when he was gone, removed his battered felt hat and passed it to me.

"Hide that," he said. "Hide it anywhere. Anywhere you like, feller. Upstairs or downstairs. Don't make a particle of dif'rence."

I took the hat and looked about for an unlikely place to deposit it. The storekeeper stood in his doorway, surveying with mild interest the pair of lunatics before him.

"May I hide this in your store?" I asked.

He seemed the least bit doubtful, wondering, I suppose, if we had homicidal tendencies.

"You hide it," I suggested. "Somewhere in the store where the dog can't find it."

I held it out to him, and after a moment he took it gingerly by the rim and went inside. We heard him rummaging about among boxes and barrels, but he emerged presently.

"I've hid it," he said, "but they's some things about this I don't understand."

I explained. "The dog is a very fine retriever, and I am trying to hide the hat where he can't find it."

"Well, I guess you needn't worry," he drawled, "but

[66]

what I don't understand is what hurt would it do if he did find it."

"Pedro!"

The call and the rush of the dog coming in saved me the bother of trying to explain.

The stranger had collapsed again on the lower step, and now as the dog came up and thrust his muzzle within the circling fold of his master's arm, that incomparable trainer raised his voice in melancholy lament.

"Ish a dark night, Pedro, and we're a hunderd miles from home. Ish a dark night and ish raining, and I've lost my chapeau, Pedro, I've lost my chapeau. Oh what'll we do, Pedro? What *will* we do?"

That glorious pointer thrust his muzzle upward, gave the tear-stained face above him a loving lick with his tongue, backed out from the encircling arm, and started off. Around the road he went and back to us, passed behind us and up over the store steps, went by the open door without looking in, came down, and made another longer circle. Back again he came and once more went up the steps and past the door.

Then, for the first time, I saw him retrace his steps. He turned about, came back to the doorway, and looked in. He sniffed the air eagerly for a moment, then edged past the staring storekeeper and went inside.

We listened to the pad of his feet on the floor. Presently they ceased. There was a moment of silence and then the sudden clatter of overturned boxes—and he came out with the hat in his mouth.

"I hid it in an empty cracker box behind the counter and put a cover over it," said the storekeeper. "Don't it beat all?"

I asked my question.

"What system did you use in training him?"

He placed the battered hat on his head, threw his arm around the pointer's neck, and drew him close.

"I'll tell you," he said. "Yeshsir, I'll tell you all about it. We're brothers, see? I'm his brother an' he's my brother. When I talk to him, I talk to him jush like a brother. Tha's all there is to it."

I picked up my gun, and with the setter at heel, trudged homeward. As I walked, I thought of the thousands of bird dogs to be trained that fall. I thought of the myriads of puppies yet unborn. And then it occurred to me that this system, practiced by such a pitiful few, was not such a bad one after all.

CHAPTER VI

MY good friend Teel was a woodcock fiend. In those halcyon days when we hunted much together, he regarded woodcock with the same amount of enthusiasm I entertained for grouse. The only differences we ever had were caused by that.

We might be—and, in fact, were on many occasions—in the very midst of a large flock of grouse when a woodcock would go up. If he were in the range of Teel's gun, the day was not marred by any unpleasantness excepting such slight physical discomfort as the woodcock might momentarily know, for my friend was an exceptionally good shot.

Such was not always the case, for occasionally the little russet feller flushed out of range. Then pandemonium broke loose. Did we continue hunting the grouse that were scattered all about us? Most emphatically we did not. The dog was called in, and we proceeded to move heaven and earth to find that woodcock. If we found him, well and good. Teel would gloat over him for a minute or so, stroking the exquisite coat, and gradually the light of reason would come back in his eyes. Then he would pocket the bird, and we would go back to the really important business of the day.

I loved dearly to hunt woodcock with him—but not in grouse country. He understood the birds so well, knew so exactly, on his first time through it, whether or not a covert was "right" for them, and if it were, in what part of it we would find them. It was a liberal education just to follow along beside him and listen to his words of wisdom. I wish I had met him earlier in life. Then I might have avoided that mortifying experience I had with woodcock in my youth.

For a season or two I had been killing an occasional grouse on the wing, and although no one had ever mentioned it to me, I had somehow become imbued with the idea that I was "the eel's eyebrows." Woodcock had been entirely beneath my dignity. I had no interest in them whatsoever and did not hunt the coverts they frequented. For me grouse was king, but when a youth of my acquaintance told me there was a tremendous flight of woodcock in the Walker pasture, I paused long enough to listen to the siren song. It seemed that he had been shooting at them for several days, and that shooting had been errorless. Not a single mistake to snuff out, in an instant, the life of a harmless little woodcock.

I listened with tolerant amusement while my youthful brain tried to solve the problem presented. Grouse were the hardest of all targets. I could kill grouse—occasionally.

Woodcock were comparatively easy. Why, the problem solved itself. I could kill woodcock as fast as they got up.

"I'll go up there tomorrow morning and knock over fifteen or twenty of them," I promised, with all the egotism in the world. Woodcock! Huh! Why, there's absolutely nothing to it.

Sunrise the next morning found me entering the Walker pasture, my chest swelling with self-esteem, my pockets bulging with shells.

The bars at the gate were down, and as I stepped over them, three woodcock went up simultaneously from the sunny side of the stone wall beside me. I recall now that I felt a slight irritation at their method of departure. No booming wing beats to attract the attention; no sudden miniature whirlwind of autumn leaves behind them. They merely bounced straight up, with a faint whistling sound, and even as I gazed, spellbound, were gone.

Consoling myself with the adage concerning a poor beginning and a good ending, I started in pursuit. The beginning was bad enough to satisfy the most superstitious of persons. At nine o'clock I started homeward, minus one box of shells and plus absolutely nothing but a saddening experience. Taking on another full cargo of munitions, I ate a sandwich and went back to the field of battle.

The engagement which followed has lasted more than

twenty-five years; yet I cannot truthfully say I have ever found woodcock an easy mark. Theoretically they are just that, but I am still prone to miss the easiest of shots.

Indeed!!

My observation of grouse leads me to believe they possess a certain amount of reasoning power. Once they have perfected a plan they try to carry it through.

The woodcock, to the contrary, seems devoid of brains. His mechanism appears to be a tremendous spring, wound to the last, ultimate cog. At what moment it will release and propel him upward twenty feet in the air, neither he, my dog, nor myself knows.

He may bounce into the air before the dog comes to a point, so far away that only the upthrust muzzle warns me of the flight; he may lie to a point and rise as I come up, giving me the perfect shot I carelessly miss so often; or he may lie so near the dog that I can tell, by the down-pointing muzzle, he is but a few feet from those quivering nostrils.

Then I may stand at my dog's side and scan the ground for minutes before I see him. His little shoe-button eyes betray him. They are invariably the first things I see, for his protective coloration is the masterpiece of a Master Artist. If I let my glance stray for a moment, I have to look for those eyes again. From them I can trace his outline plainly as he squats among the autumn leaves, his head drawn back upon his body and his flexible bill resting upon the ground.

[72]

Is he alarmed at our close proximity? Apparently not, for he sits there, unblinking, supremely confident of his invisibility.

I call my companion and he comes crashing through the brush to stand at my side. We talk together and the little chap knows no alarm. If we speak of his beauty, he will, quite often, arise and stretch his wings stiffly downward as he lifts them slightly from his sides. At the same time he tips his tail straight upward and spreads it, fanwise, in exactly the same gesture a turkey gobbler uses during the mating season. He struts a few proud steps and pirouettes about, as our fingers reach for the safeties, then settles, abruptly, down in the leaves once more.

We debate whether to kick him out or to leave him for another day and, while we are talking, without the slightest warning movement, some invisible, inside force propels him skyward like a miniature rocket. On such occasions, I truthfully admit, we most often place him on the list of those to be looked up on the way out.

A woodcock will spring up so suddenly before you that no one could convince you he did not intend flying at least a half mile. Then, ere he has reached the tops of the alders, he will change the thing which operates in place of his mind and drop, unconcernedly, back to earth. The roar of your gun and the hissing of shot through the atmosphere, where he was a split second before, makes not the slightest differ-ence. He will alight and sit as dumbly as a wooden Indian, not even wondering what it is all about.

All this is unjust, and no one knows it better than I. He is a gamy little fellow, going his cocksure way, and he has my admiration and respect.

It is surprising that he is so little known, so seldom seen by those who do not hunt him. Many an out-of-doors man has said to me, "I don't know that I ever saw a live wood-cock in my life."

My friend Teel was tramping homeward one night with his pointer at heel. They were tired but happy, for the limit of woodcock had been taken that day.

The way was long, the country road hilly, and when a farmer overtook them, pulled his horse to a halt and asked if he could give them a lift, Teel accepted, gratefully.

"Did you get anything?" the farmer asked.

"We had a great time today," said Teel. "We took the limit of woodcock."

"Woodcock? Woodcock? I don't know as I ever see a woodcock."

Teel extracted one from his shooting coat and exhibited it, proudly. The farmer took it, turned it over in his hand, and looked at it long and thoughtfully.

"So that's a woodcock, is it?" he said. "Well, if you like

to hunt them critters, I just wisht you could have been up to my place this morning. That elm tree out in front of my house was full of 'em."

The knowledge of the uninitiated, concerning the habits and habitat of the little russet fellow, seems to be about on a par with that of the farmer. Yet the woodcock has a wider range than the ruffed grouse, flourished in countless thousands, in years past and, thanks to wise legislation, is again increasing rapidly.

I wish I knew more about them. There are many things concerning their habits which still remain a mystery to me.

Within a mile of my home there is an exceptionally good woodcock covert. There are several hundred acres in it and, to me, the ground, the trees and the underbrush seem the same on every acre of it. There are no particular spots in it where a woodcock hunter, who was unacquainted with the territory, could say "Here, if anywhere, we will find birds." Yet within that large area are about a dozen spots where you are certain to find them if any are in the covert. Native birds feed there and, when the flight is on, big, heavy birds from the north drop in to these same spots. I can understand why birds reared in that section could learn that here they could gain their sustenance more easily, but how do the flight birds know it?

Unlike most coverts with which I am familiar, these

spots remain good year after year. Usually a certain, well-favored corner will go "sour" after a year or two, and the birds leave it for some place which better suits their rather finical taste.

Quite often what has been regarded as an extremely good feeding ground will be vacated by the birds and shunned for several seasons when, to my eye, it possesses exactly the same characteristics it has had since I first knew it.

This recalls an amusing incident which happened several years ago. It is amusing now, after a lapse of a few years, but was not painfully humorous at the time it happened.

A relative of an intimate friend came into town, armed to the teeth, his car sagging with the weight of his ammunition and a pair of businesslike bird dogs.

The friend introduced us without loss of time. It developed, after a few minutes spent in admiring his dogs, that he was here for the duration of the woodcock season and would appreciate being shown some of our best coverts.

Had the proposed duration of his stay been shorter, his request would have met with infinitely greater favor; but my shooting companion and I had tramped many weary miles to find some of these favored spots, and somehow we just couldn't visualize a stranger, with a car and two dogs, taking the cream of the shooting for the next thirty days.

Steve and I went into conference.

"Where shall we take him?" I asked.

"I don't know," said Steve, "but I know d—n well where we won't. If he hunts the Hollow or the School-house cover or the Pray pasture, it'll be over my dead body."

"Why not take him over to the Milliard Brook? That's big enough to satisfy him, and it certainly is a sweet-looking covert. It will keep him occupied for a few days, and by that time we will have thought of some other places."

The Milliard Brook territory was a very beautiful covert, but we had crossed it off the map two years before. It was extensive enough for an all-day hunt and it would delight the eye of any woodcock enthusiast, but for some unknown reason the birds had practically abandoned it.

The idea won Steve's instant favor. We adjourned the conference, bundled into the stranger's sedan, and piloted him to the Milliard Brook Covert, chuckling in our sleeves like the knaves we were.

It was a good joke—but it was on us. We took him over the whole territory and the place literally teemed with 'cock. Both dogs were almost continuously on point, and he went from one to the other, like a besieged Pilgrim in a blockhouse, firing at the dancing redskins from alternate portholes.

When the sun had set, we called in the dogs and together we proceeded to take an inventory. Of his original
fifty shells fourteen remained. He had three woodcock,
one of which was a wing-tipped bird which a dog had
brought in and for which we credited him with an assist.

We drove homeward in the gathering dusk; Steve on
the back seat, morose and silent, between two tired dogs;
the stranger still agitated but so eloquent he was almost
lyric as he lauded that covert to the star-sprinkled skies; I
with queer convulsions disturbing my diaphragm, and
longing to shout, in loud and unrestrained laughter, as the
humor of the situation seized me.

We let him have the covert to himself that fall, and he
claimed to have taken the season limit from it. I do not
doubt it. Even after seeing him shoot on that memorable
afternoon, I can still credit his statement. There were birds
enough for several limits, and he had a carload of ammunition—when he came. Yes, despite all, I believe he told the
truth.

It has always seemed to me that I can kill grouse more
easily and more consistently than I can woodcock. I do not
mean that from a given number of birds of each species
flushed I would score a greater percentage of hits on
grouse, but I always feel that a close and comparatively
open shot at the larger bird is an absolutely certain hit.

With the smaller fellow, something within me says when he crumples in the air, "Well, you did hit that one."

Reason tells me it is merely a matter of timing. I am keyed up for a fast one, and old Timberdoodle lobs one of those disconcerting fade-away balls over the plate. If I discover it in time, I can drive it into the bleachers, but, too often for my egotism, I swing too hard and too soon.

A French Canadian friend convinced me concerning the matter of timing. He had a way with dogs that I liked. He was so gently-firm and so trust-inspiring that his dogs seemed to obey his unspoken thoughts. He also had a way with guns which was diametrically opposed to the laws of ballistics, my own ideas, and all orthodox principles.

It was he who, unknown to me, caught his toe on a root and pitched headlong, driving his gun, muzzle first, inches deep in the soft earth. A few minutes later when a rabbit dashed out of a brush-heap, he swung the gun in that general direction and, as he invariably did when excited, pulled both triggers simultaneously.

The bursting barrels and the doubly hard recoil put him prone upon his back. Instantly he scrambled to his feet, rubbing his shoulder as he did so, and looked down on the ruined gun.

"By Gar! I know when that go off!" he said.

We had hunted together for several days and, at last,

just as dusk was falling, a fat old woodcock arose before him and, circling, gave him a perfect cross-shot. There were four separate entities concerned with the episode; he, the woodcock, the dog, and myself. Of the four, only the woodcock remained unsurprised, and it was the fact of his being dead which prevented his sharing our feelings. It was a remarkably clean kill and Latour was elated.

"I'm a son-of-a-gun," he cried. "I'm a son-of-a-gun! Now I know what I do all this time. I don't point my gun on him."

I told him I was aware of that, but he seemed not to hear me.

"She's easy like rolling off a tree," he exulted. "I been hurry too much. I think all the time those woodcock go *whiz-z-z*. That's wrong for sure. She just go *purr-r-r*."

He raised his gun deliberately and swung it in a slow arc which included my hatband.

"Like that she go," he told me. "If I shoot ten woodcock tomorrow I hit nine of them, I bet you. What you say?"

I said it was quite likely. I said undoubtedly he had discovered the correct system. I said I would like to see that system operate. I said we would go tomorrow.

We went, and by careful manipulation I succeeded in giving him seventeen good shots and several hard ones. He accepted each and every chance, and ruffled not one solitary feather for the day.

In the end he grinned charmingly, accepting defeat without rancor.

"Those woodcock, she's funny feller," he confided to me. "Yesterday I hurry an' all day he go *purr-r-r*. Today I go *purr-r-r* an' she go *whiz-z-z*. He's little son-of-a-gun."

It is not for me to censor the applied epithet, for on various occasions I have called the little fellow that, and worse. He is so versatile in his manner of flight, so prone to do the unconventional thing that it is often quite disconcerting. He is an artist in putting one in a state of mind that is conducive of poor shooting, especially so when he "struts his stuff" on the ground before taking wing.

It is with keen enjoyment I recall an afternoon when four of us met in an open field and started across to a covert on the other side.

One of the party was a young Croesus. His clothes were the mould of fashion, his gun the work of a master craftsman. Despite the fact of his youth he was not a novice at the shooting game and had acquitted himself creditably during the morning.

His physique was excellent, his sight and hearing of the best, nor was he handicapped by an inferiority complex.

[81]

Personally I had come to believe the things he said of himself were true, and I could see Doc warming up to him gradually. Only Steve remained unconvinced, gloomily taciturn and restrained, confining his contribution to the conversation to noncommittal grunts.

Halfway across the field was a little patch of bushes not more than ten feet across. Passing the edge of this, one of the dogs suddenly wheeled and pointed staunchly, while the other came up and honored his point.

The young Nimrod advanced to the very edge of the brush, directly ahead of the dog, and peered in through the leafy screen.

"It's a woodcock," he called. "I can see him on the ground." He backed away a step and glanced at the surrounding country—the little patch of bushes waist-high, the open field, the surrounding wood several hundred yards away.

"Fellows," he said, "that woodcock stands exactly the same chance of survival that a snowball would have in Hades."

For the first time in hours Steve spoke intelligibly.

"Do you think you could take him?" he asked.

"For one dollar or five," boasted the youngster.

"Make it ten, and I'll kick him out for you," snapped Steve.

"Done," said the youth and proceeded to slip two extra shells into his pump. With that gesture of doubt I knew Steve had a chance to be in on the money. He came in softly to the edge of the brush and then leaped crashingly into it.

The result was as he had planned. The bird came out fast and low, straight at the young fellow's face. He ducked to let it pass, and whirling, emptied five shells into the surrounding atmosphere.

He stared after the unhurt bird until it reached the shelter of the distant wood, then slid the gun under his arm and reached for his pocketbook.

"I guess it doesn't pay to be too confident," he said. "Here's your ten."

"Oh, hell," said Steve. "We all miss 'em occasionally. Keep your money, kid."

A medical friend of mine, who is also a scientist, relates the story of a woodcock that gave him one of the great surprises of an eventful life.

Being interested to know just how keen was the olfactory organ of a present-day human, Doc decided to make some practical tests. Accordingly, the next time his dog made a staunch point on grouse, he crept up and, dropping flat on his stomach, wormed his way past the dog. Inch by inch he pushed himself ahead until at last he was rewarded by being able to smell the grouse distinctly.

He was successful on several similar occasions, but one day, with the dog indicating that the bird was very near and with the wind in absolutely the right direction, he was unable to detect the slightest odor. Baffled, he crept about through the brush, seeking the elusive scent, his face a few scant inches from Mother Earth.

Suddenly a very gamy smell assailed his nostrils and, in that instant, a woodcock burst into action under his very nose.

"You can imagine the start it gave me," said Doc; "the wings hammering my face and beating dirt into my eyes. But I convinced myself that I could smell them, and now I let the dog do it."

That there is some sense which warns certain people of the proximity of game I am fully convinced. A cardinal rule of the successful hunter is: "Never be taken by surprise." The thought that you are hunting and game may start at any moment should always be uppermost in one's mind. I have always tried to observe the rule, and it is seldom the unexpected rise of a grouse or woodcock finds me unprepared; but hundreds of times in my life something within me has said, "Go to the right," or "Go to the left," or "Go to the other side of that evergreen" and, on doing so, I have found a bird there. I may have unconsciously smelled them, I may have known the location was ideal, or I may have failed to remember the many times I have been wrong. I merely know that quite often I am right.

One gets to know the birdy-looking places only by experience and close observation of conditions.

If, after a hot and dry summer, some covert is plentifully supplied with woodcock, it is reasonable to suppose that another place of the same character will contain birds also.

Reason and supposition are not infallible, however. One of my most memorable recollections of perfect woodcock shooting was on a bit of ground that not even a novice would have given a second glance. We crossed it, by necessity, to get to a favorable bit of lowland which lay beyond. The ground in question had been a pine clad side hill the year before but had been stripped the previous winter. It had a southern slope and was of a springy nature, but I had never found woodcock on stripped lots before and never expect to again.

We had started across the clearing, by one of the numerous paths between the windrows of brush, and had gone but a little way before the dog pointed. We went in, expecting a straying grouse, and were surprised when a woodcock emerged from the brush-pile. I killed the bird, pocketed it, and we started on, thinking merely that this was an unusual place to find even a lone woodcock. Halfway across the clearing the dog again came to another point. Still, dumbly, expecting a grouse we went in and again a woodcock arose. I garnered this one also and we went on, all unmindful of the possibilities in those brush-piles around us. Before we reached the edge of the wood, which was our objective, we had flushed the third bird, which also fell to me.

It was then Gene awoke to the fact that here was something which should be investigated. Tersely he explained the sort of fools we were, and suggested nay, commanded, we take another path back through the brush-heaps.

We went back and I added another bird to my collection. Back again through another road and I missed one and bagged two, giving me what was then the daily limit of six. As yet Gene had failed to connect, for only one bird had presented him with a possible shot.

Feeling quite a philanthropist now that I had reached my quota, I began driving birds to Gene. He is a first-class bird hunter, but occasionally has "another one of those days." This chanced to be one of them. Quickly realizing the fact, woodcock from the uncombed portions of that cut-off, and from other coverts within sound of the bombardment, came flocking to the scene with all the eager animation of children going to a circus. They flew before him in singles, in pairs—yes, even in triples—and the gun missed them with equal impartiality.

The psychological effect was too much for Gene, and his average, which had been zero at first, became rapidly worse.

His education was gained far from the waterfront, yet he has acquired a vocabulary with which, in times of stress like these, he could hold a 'longshoreman spellbound.

The air about him became faintly bluish in color, while leaves on the succulent new shoots, in his immediate vicinity, trembled violently and withered as with a searing blast. But all to no avail. Strangely meek, he called, at last, for help.

"We're entitled to twelve woodcock," he said; "but if we get them, you'll have to kill them. I can't hit the-bad-word-things."

Now here is a queer thing. I had just taken six out of seven chances, which is a little better than 85% and is, for me, considerably above top form. I had absolute confidence in my ability that day. I had not the handicap of being behind in my score and anxious to catch up. I know of no reason why I should not have killed the next bird that got up, but I did not, nor the next, nor the next.

A growing feeling of apprehension made itself apparent

within my consciousness. My supply of shells was running low, and to add to my discomfiture, Gene began laughing at me, a hoarse guffaw, when I missed birds I might well have hit with a stone.

Laughter was the panacea he needed, however, for he took his next shot cleanly, whereupon I, ammunitionless at last, watched in admiration while he took his limit without a miss.

Those are the things which make the shooting game the fascinating sport it is.

CHAPTER VII

DID you ever sigh for the good old days of the Pilgrim Forefathers, when a man could go out and, in a few hours, shoot a backload of upland game? It undoubtedly was a pleasurable experience, but I'll wager no stern and sturdy old Puritan ever did that little trick without wishing, with all his heart, he might have hunted before "ye damme sauvages" had ruined the shooting.

I'll wager also that the day's hunt, although interesting, was a nerve-racking experience. The old boy started out light, his sole sporting equipment being his powder-horn, his shot-pouch, his rest and his matchlock, his flint and steel, and a supply of fuses.

His method of procedure was simplicity itself. When he neared the vicinity of game, he stopped and struck a fire with his flint and steel, and ignited his slow match. With that glowing to his satisfaction, he proceeded until the game was sighted and within range. Then he laid his eighteen-pound blunderbuss on the ground and sought out a place in Mother Earth where the ground was sufficiently soft to enable him to set up his rest, a crotched stick with a tapering point which he pushed deep into the soil. With that set to his liking, he hoisted the blunderbuss into the crotch, pointed it as best he could with the bell muzzle cutting a large area from his visibility, then, holding it against his shoulder and keeping it pointed with one hand, he inserted the slow match in the hole in the breach and, with bated breath and a muttered prayer, awaited results.

That they should be forthcoming was inevitable, for the game was there before him; but again, I will wager that, for him, the greatest kick he got out of it was from the steel-shod butt of that old blunderbuss.

To be sure, I would like to go back to those glorious times for a little while, but it must be specified in the contract that I may leave at any moment I choose. If the thing should suddenly get too cloying, I reserve the privilege to quit.

For years I have been an ardent trout fisherman. Put me on a bit of good water, with plenty of room for my back cast, and leave me alone. I'll be back in a week or so, hungry and tired, without any fish—but happy. Just last year it was my privilege to fish a glorious stream that flirted with the Canadian border. With the family I had driven three hundred miles the day before—a full hundred more than I care to negotiate in one day—solely that I might be at a certain favorite pool on that stream by daybreak the next morning.

Dawn found me knee-deep in the pool, conning my fly-book for the first offering to the speckled beauties which were feeding all over the surface of the pool.

Yes, there was I—save for my modern equipment a primal man—gazing down on what might well have been virgin water, for hundreds of hungry trout were there before my eyes.

I thought of the family, still sweetly sleeping in camp, and laid my plans accordingly. I would first make sure of a good dinner for them—four worth-while trout of approximately a foot in length. Then I would abandon myself to such an orgy of trout fishing as the average fisherman only dreams of. I would play those speckled beauties to the limit of their endurance, and when they had given up the battle, I would release them gently and hook another fresh fighter.

It was eight hours until noon. For seven of them I would cast and fight fish until my rod assumed a permanent bow and my tired fingers could no longer retrieve line. Then, saturated to my very soul with enjoyment, I would quit.

I took my four fish, rejecting and selecting until they suited my fancy. That was business; and now for sport. Already I had taken several doubles, but they fought against each other and I felt they were robbing me of my just dues.

[91]

I changed leaders and used a single fly. The trout were voracious and took it too readily, whereupon I changed to one of a less gaudy pattern.

They liked that equally as well, so I changed to dries. But it was of no avail, and in exactly one hour and thirty minutes those trout, by their very plentifulness, drove me from the brook.

Looking back at it now, I realize that the sole pleasure I derived from that experience was in the manner of their taking, the play of the little rod, and the judging to an ounce what the light leader would stand. There could have been no satisfaction in sweeping the pool with a drag-net or shattering its placid surface with dynamite. What joy there was in the incident came from using good tools and using them well.

So it is with shooting. The days of big bags are forever past; and yet there is unmeasured joy in store for the countless thousands who will tread the gold and crimson forests for untold years to come.

Of those countless thousands some will be doubly fortunate. They will be the thoughtful youths who early learn that there is more joy in one fast, difficult kill than in a dozen easy ones that a tyro could emulate. They will be men who know guns and dogs and will be satisfied with nothing less than the best of each.

Were you ever galvanized into sudden startled action at the whir-r-r of a rising bird, and realize even as you swing about, with the gun coming to your shoulder, that this, if successful, would be a split-second affair, for the grouse has but a scant ten feet to go to reach the haven of a leafy screen and safety? Did you ever have your muscles respond, in one lightning burst of speed, to the command of your will, and know in that last, glorious moment when the bird was disappearing from view and your shoulder was absorbing the recoil, that you had judged all the factors in that momentary drama with absolute accuracy?

If you have not known such a glorious moment, you have missed much from life. If you have known it, then you are reaping your reward for the care and thoughtfulness with which you selected your scatter-gun, and the hours and dollars you spent in making it a part of your very anatomy, rather than an awkward and clumsy bit of iron and wood.

To one not experienced in the art, shots like these seem miraculous, a chance thing that could happen only once or twice in a lifetime; yet a good bird hunter does it many, many times throughout the season, and curses his carelessness when he misses.

"You must be getting old," he challenges the inner being which is himself. "You saw that bird, in the clear, for a good ten feet. What is the matter with you? Paralyzed or something?"

The tyro will invariably say, "Oh, he's just naturally gifted that way," but he was never more mistaken. The good shot must, of necessity, be gifted with excellent sight and hearing; but coördination of muscle and will, the judging of speed and distance, and the delicate art of placing a charge of shot where the will dictates, are only acquired by years of persistent and persevering practice.

If you doubt the accuracy of this statement, pause long enough to make the following experiment: Take a table fork, of the pattern you like best, in your master hand. Bend the other arm until the fingers rest upon the shoulder. Then, with head elevated, place the points of the fork exactly on the center of your protruding elbow bone. Ha-Ha! I thought so. Yet I would not be afraid to wager you could hit your mouth with it quite consistently, even with your eyes closed—and you could hit your elbow as well, if you had practiced it as much and with the same enthusiasm.

Were I beginning again, as I once did, to fit myself for a lifetime of bird shooting, I would buy—as soon as I could beg, borrow or steal the money—a gun built to fit my individual requirements and of a quality to last a lifetime. It would be manufactured under the flag to which I owed allegiance, and bear the stamp of a maker upon whose integrity I could rely. Then, after it was mine, I would devote ten years of daily practice to making it as much a part of my being as the fingers on my hands. I would shoot it when I could, but I would devote hours and weeks and months in handling it—throwing it up with what speed I could possibly obtain at stationary objects, alternating from one to the other, and pausing momentarily to verify my judgment. I would do that until the gun was worn bright and shiny— and the nerves of the better half were worn to that thin edge where she would hysterically cry, "For goodness sake, will you stop pointing that thing around the room and sit down for a minute!"

Probably I would again be human enough to imagine that faultless bit of artistry was not exactly suited to my requirements; and I would waste priceless years in alternating from one gun to another, trying to find that fabulous and fondly imagined bit of mechanism which automatically and unerringly pointed itself. Then, with shattered ideals and the wisdom of middle age, I would settle down to one gun and find, very shortly, I was shooting better than ever before in my hectic life.

Occasionally a man is so elongated or compressed that he cannot be fitted with one of the many dimensions which are standard in good guns, but it is a rare occurrence. In most cases, by persistent practice, one can accustom himself to a weapon of average dimensions and shoot creditably.

I have a friend who suffered an injury to his left eye after he had become a rather good wing shot. He was hopelessly left-handed, and after the accident, began shooting left-handed as of old, but with the gun butt at his right shoulder. Personally, I have never tried anything which impressed me as being so hard to do, but he did it and did it well. Then, several years ago, he bought an automatic, and because the ejected shells often jammed against his cramped right fore-arm, he changed to a straight right-handed shooter. It has cost him considerable time and money, but he had the will to conquer and he has made gloriously good.

In the course of my lifetime I have had guns built to meet what I fondly imagined were my especial requirements. They were good guns, but they have gone into other hands, and for the last fifteen years my pet has been a gun whose measurements could be duplicated in any first-class sporting-goods store. The gun fits me well, in fact, I know of no change I would have made if I were ordering another. I shoot it, however, much better than I did when it was new. The years have mellowed it and have robbed it of much of its original value, but they have done something else. They have welded into one complete unit that old gun and the correlated muscles of mine that control it. There is no conscious effort on my part in pointing it and the charge lands where my brain wills it to. The gun and my muscular action are faultless. The errors are the fault of that laggard brain of mine which fails to judge, accurately and instantaneously, the speed, distance and angle of flight of the bird at which I shot.

This gives rise to another thought.

Many a time and oft, I have heard a man condemn his gun to the realm of the unquenchable conflagration, when the fault was entirely his own. A few shots at a square of paper, large enough to receive the entire charge, would soon convince him of that.

Every bird hunter should properly target his gun in this manner. It not only gives him confidence in his weapon but it helps fix in his mind the distance at which, with given sizes of shot, he may reasonably expect to kill game. At greater distances than these, it is unwise to shoot.

At a distance of thirty yards, a 12 gauge, cylinder bore, should cover a thirty-inch circle, with 8s or 9s, so thoroughly and evenly that no openings are left through which a grouse could pass without being hard hit. With a full choke the same effect should be produced at an added distance of approximately ten yards. That is a fair average. Some guns will exceed this and some few will fail to measure up to that standard. With the latter, I would experiment with various loads of powder and shot. Then, if the pattern was still unsatisfactory, I would, with as much honesty as is consistent with gun trading, exchange it for one of a better grade.

There is a great amount of satisfaction in owning a good gun and gracefully growing old with it.

I have a Parker that has been with me for a long time. I have come, through the years, to think of it, not as my Parker, but by the phrase they have made famous, "The Old Reliable."

For more than a score of years this gun never did a wrong thing, and then, one day—

Count roaded up through the brush ahead of me and pointed, staunchly, straight toward an old stone wall which lay twenty yards ahead.

It was an ideal spot for grouse. I slipped off the safety and went, carefully, ahead. Beyond the wall was a bit of stripped land and, when I had worked through the brush and come within a score of feet of the weed and juniper covered wall, I knew that any bird, rising within range, would have a poor chance of winning clear.

Then Count loosened up on his point, worked in to the wall, jumped it, roaded out into the stripped lot for ten yards and, again, pointed staunchly.

I worked up to the wall, slid the gun back under my

arm, scrambled quickly over the tottering rocks, gained a solid footing on the other side and gave the gun the little forward flip with my forearm which propels it into my hands.

In that instant, there came a deafening roar which almost shattered my eardrums, dirt and sticks flew from the ground ahead of me and I found myself holding The Old Reliable by the muzzle while I looked, dazedly, about to see what damage had been done.

No one, unless he has had a similar experience, will ever know the feelings that were mine. It was not fright but, rather, a dreadful sense of apprehension; a feeling that I had been betrayed. Exactly the same sensation might be felt by a man who, on arriving home, should learn that the wife of his bosom, whom he had loved and cherished for years, had eloped with the chauffeur, the iceman, or some other nonentity who had caught her momentary fancy.

I was at a loss to discover the cause. No amount of jarring would cause the hammer to slip again. Releasing the safety, I hammered the butt on the ground until reason told me to stop—and still no slip. That the day was spoiled I knew, so I went, sadly, home and took the gun apart. The mechanism, after more than twenty years of use, was absolutely perfect. No part showed the slightest wear. It was mechanically impossible for the gun to discharge unless the trigger was pulled, yet the thing had happened. There was no denying that fact.

The next day I chose another gun, but I could not dismiss the incident from my mind. I knew there must, somewhere, be a cause for each effect, and it intrigued me that I could not determine the cause for this one.

Becoming reconciled, at last, to the fact that this must have been one of the things which can happen but once in a lifetime, I began using the Parker once more, but I made a mental vow to never again release the safety until the bird flushed. Why I ever do otherwise I do not know, for I always, instinctively, go through the mechanical operation, even when I know it is off.

For a few days nothing happened. Then, with the dog on point, I slid the gun forward, from its accustomed place in the hollow of my arm. It slid smoothly halfway, then came to a sudden and abrupt stop. At the same instant, something pulled, sharply, at the back of my coat.

Pulling forward failed to bring the gun ahead so I twisted about and investigated. My triumphant yell was genuine. I was happy once more. I had discovered the cause. The Old Reliable was still just that.

My shooting coat was new and I had been foolish enough to specify a button on each flap of the rear game pocket. That button was in exactly the right place, and was

of exactly the right size to button itself inside the trigger guard, and no amount of pulling forward would release it. A slight backward movement, however, would unfasten it instantly, a thing which the recoil from the accidental discharge had done, and made of the affair a mystery which I thought would never be solved. Now no debutante gives the matter of buttons more serious consideration than I.

A gun, of any type, is dangerous. Until the auto usurped the place of honor, firearms were listed, and rightly so, as the cause of more accidental deaths than any other one thing devised by the hand of man.

Accidental discharges are numerous. Almost every hunter, no matter how careful he has always been, can rate one or more of these nerve-racking experiences. It is an uncanny thing and beyond my comprehension why, with all the vast universe around it where it might roam until it dropped from sheer physical exhaustion, an unexpected, unpremeditated and unwanted charge of shot will, almost invariably, choose to travel in the one direction it should not.

Neither have I ever been able to fathom why a city chap, whose woodcraft has been gained solely in some arboretum and whose lack of gun knowledge is only equaled by his lack of common sense, can go into the big woods, convince himself that a guide, three hundred yards distant,

[101]

is a deer, and blow his brains out with a celerity and unfailing precision which Buffalo Bill in his palmy days could not have equaled.

In my lifetime I have hunted with a great many people, but as time rolls on I find that list is impervious to inflation. In fact, it grows smaller with the passing years.

Undoubtedly it is a mental weakness, like the magnified dread of the dentist's forceps, but I have a growing horror of stopping a young and spirited charge of shot with any portion of my anatomy. Possibly it may not be such a tremendously unpleasant sensation; in fact, I have been told that the swiftly traveling bits of lead act as a local anesthetic and there is very little pain. I am willing to believe that, or any other reasonable hypothesis, so long as I am not elected to judge the matter personally.

I have seen men suffering from gunshot wounds and the sight is one not easily forgotten. One recollection which still remains vivid, after a quarter century, is that of a man sitting on his doorstep and giving himself first aid for a charge of No. 6s in the calf of his leg.

He was of that type which Darwin would have given his all to find; a living prototype of the missing link. The theory has been advanced that animals of this species suffer no physical or mental emotions. Not so. This chap sat on his own doorstep, his undershot jaw grating against his upper incisors while, with a not too sharp or overly clean pocket knife, he sawed at the skin on the inner side of his muscular calf, just over a protruding bunch the size of an English walnut. That bunch was one and one-eighth ounces of shot, together with the debris it had collected in its passage through that four inches of muscle.

I remember, too, a remarkable phenomenon which I witnessed, for the first time in my life, on that occasion. A strange and terrifying darkness was suddenly before my eyes, as though the sun had been blotted out by a mighty hand. The earth reeled like a drunken gyroscope, while a deadly nausea assailed me.

I kept my feet with difficulty while, with what will power remained, I strove to reason the thing away. It passed, after a time, but there must have been much of interest that I lost. The shot were out, a gory handful of them, lying on one of the steps, and that primordial creature was swabbing the wound with a drab colored handkerchief saturated with shellac.

I am advancing no theory, neither am I recommending shellac as a panacea. It was his system, not mine, but it worked beautifully. No complications occurred; no blood poisoning; no gangrene. Just a clean, natural healing of the shredded muscles.

If, perchance, any of my medical friends doubt my veracity, they are cordially invited to come to me for proof. We will drive down to his home, through a score of miles of glorious grouse and woodcock country, and then, if the afternoon chances to be warm and sunny, I'll point him out, pridefully, where he swings, somnolently, from a stalwart branch of his family tree.

My good friend Hartley was as careful as any man with whom I have hunted. No weapon of his ever pointed, even momentarily, at a human being. He was familiar with guns of various types and should have been one of the last men in the world to have an accident, yet a few grains of dense smokeless nearly caused his death, and mine.

In those days, every dyed-in-the-wool gun crank had a set of reloading tools for each gun he owned and pinned his faith in that ammunition which was the product of his own little factory. He took no one's word that a certain cartridge contained a given charge and was not content unless he had measured it with his own hands.

Smokeless powder was coming into its own at that time and various theories were advanced as to its efficacy. The customary method of testing a gun for any new powder was to load a shell with a generous overcharge, slip it into the gun and tie the gun to a tree or fence post. The trigger was pulled with the aid of a long string, running to some convenient barricade. If the gun stood the ordeal, it was rated

A No. 1, and its owner felt no apprehension in using that brand of powder.

Hartley had experimented with the product of many powder manufacturers, in his heavy old rifle, and it had come through with flying colors. Not one screw had loosened and the mechanism worked as smoothly as it did on the day he took it from the store.

We had started on a big game hunt in the Maine woods and had stopped in Portland to outfit. One of Hartley's purchases was a can of Laflin and Rand's "Lightning." That was a mighty nice powder but it was a new one to us. There were certain rules and regulations, concerning the use of this concentrated dynamite, with which we were unfamiliar but we learned them, shortly, with a thoroughness that was laudable.

On the first morning in camp, Hartley expressed his intention of loading a box of shells with the new powder and testing the old gun for trajectory and penetration.

We swaged and reprimed twenty brass cases and he began filling them. Each shell was filled to overflowing, struck once, then leveled off evenly at the top of the case. A standard, black-powder charge. Can you visualize it?

Some faint glimmering of reason stirred within me as he filled the sixth shell, and I suggested that, as neither of us knew the strength of the powder, it might be wise to load a few with lighter charges, varying the amount until, by the recoil, we might judge what was a maximum load. We voted on the matter and found the result to be a tie, whereupon Hartley, being chairman of the committee, used his prerogative and cast the third and deciding ballot in favor of continuing as we were.

He did, however, compromise by swaging a half dozen bullets and, seating them in their cases, compressed that powder charge to the nth degree.

We placed the target, a short bolt sawed from a giant spruce, on a distant knoll, whittled a white spot in its center, and returned to the cabin.

Hartley inserted the shells, one after the other, in the magazine, then ejected them and passed all but one to me.

"I'll put just this one in the chamber," he said. "Then, if anything happens, they'll not explode."

He dropped the cartridge in the yawning chasm, closed the action and brought the rifle to his shoulder.

I have pondered oft, since then, on the perversity of the human race. Here was a man, possessed of more than an ordinary amount of gun sense, bullheadedly doing a thing at which reason shrieked in horror. He expected trouble to ensue, or he would not have extracted those extra shells. We knew better, both of us, but we were very young; a fact that explains much.

Strange it was, also, that I, who had never known gun-shyness, should step around the corner of the log cabin while he, standing square footed before the open doorway, looked over that rifle barrel for the last time.

The next instant a stunning explosion shattered the stillness of the November morning. It was unlike any rifle report I had ever heard. There was a tremendous depth to it, yet it was curiously flat. I remember that the first thought which flashed through my mind was that the mountain, which towered above us, had split in twain.

The next instant, something sinuous and snake-like came, uncoiling, around the corner of the cabin. My startled gaze recognized it, ere it had ceased its writhing, as the magazine spring, stretched to more than ten feet in length. I jumped hastily around the corner of the cabin. The rifle barrel lay on the ground before me, split a third of its length and rolled outward as though it were made of lead.

Hartley was nowhere in sight. I sprang to the doorway and peered within. He was still on his feet, halfway across the cabin, and weaving like a drunken sailor. He held the gunstock in his hands, as though for equilibrium. Blood was streaming from his face and running, steadily, from his square chin while, from a jagged hole in the exact center of his forehead, it spurted, with each beat of his heart, in a beautiful rainbow curve, toward me.

[107]

He was muttering deliriously, like one awakening from an anesthetic, "Is it deep? Is it deep?"

It was not. That jagged hole in the center of his forehead was but a severed artery, caused by the hammer of the gun ricocheting from his noble brow. The thousand and one bleeding places on his face were merely imbedded grains of powder.

He had gone through that momentary inferno and come out unharmed. A bucket of water and a towel, a strip or two of adhesive tape and a liberal application of iodine, made him absolutely watertight once more.

For two days he sat in the camp with a mirror the size of a silver dollar in one hand and a darning needle, which might well have been an upholsterer's pride, in the other, excavating beneath the surface of his wind tanned skin for those imbedded powder grains. On the afternoon of the third day, when the last grain was salvaged and his beauty was restored to his liking, he tucked his old shotgun under his arm, went out and killed his two deer with a celerity and neatness which I have never seen equaled.

That was grit, old man. Again I salute you.

Another friend of mine, who has a scientific complex, manufactured, on his kitchen stove, a batch of smokeless powder which was the real thing, if I may be permitted to judge. The process was simplicity itself. He first caramelized a few pounds of sugar in a frying pan, then added his nitric acid and several condiments, stirring briskly the while. When it had cooled, he crushed it with a rolling pin and took it to a gun crank friend of mine for an official test.

Now this chap was wise and he loaded his shells as a wise man should under such circumstances. He began with one drachm and worked upward by easy stages.

The 2½ drachm load was a sweet one. The pattern was perfect, the penetration good, the recoil negligible. The 2¾ drachm load unjacked a new and high grade double gun and shattered the sleepy lethargy of our village with a report which has never been equaled.

The can of powder, with what loaded shells remained, was sunk, without delay, in the deepest part of the murmuring river which lulls our townspeople to untroubled slumber.

"But these," you say, "were fool tricks. No man with a modicum of common sense would ever do such stunts as these."

That they were "fool tricks" I will agree, but they were committed by people of more than average mentality, and undoubtedly seemed to them, at the time, quite the sensible thing to do.

Did you ever draw a gun under a fence or from a car or boat with its muzzle pointed toward your mid-section?

No? Pardon me, then. No offense intended. Did you ever carry one over your shoulder with the butt forward? That is rated as a safe way to carry a gun; yet I have a friend who was twelve weeks in a hospital because he did that. He slipped, and the gun struck the ground behind him. Of course it exploded; and likewise of course, the charge shattered his leg. It always does.

Did you ever carry one the other way, with the muzzles pointing ahead? Not so good. An acquaintance has been confined, for the last twenty years, to a little six-foot plot of ground for doing that. He fell forward, the gun preceding him. He took the charge in the throat. Two inches either way would have been a clean miss, but a gun, under these circumstances, never misses. It centers the mark each time.

Did you, who have always been so careful to unload your weapon the moment you step out of the woods, ever find it loaded when you started to clean it? I have. The sensation, I wish to state, is not at all pleasing.

Did you ever see a bird suddenly start between you and another chap and fly directly toward you? That is disconcerting, and doubly so when you see the other fellow throw his gun to his shoulder and you know that nothing but instantaneous death, and possibly not that, will prevent him from pulling the trigger.

I have known that experience; known, too, the tragic lifetime of waiting for the shot to strike, and the sudden, exultant paean of thanksgiving as I realized he was such a blessedly poor shot as to miss not only the grouse, but me as well.

Have you ever thought, for one agonizing minute, you had shot a friend? I hope you may never know the numbing terror of that moment, or the nightmares that make of sleep a thing to be dreaded for months afterward.

How many shooting accidents can you list which have occurred in your community? The total of my list is appalling, and doubly so when I know they were all unnecessary. Every last one of them was caused by carelessness or a negligence that was criminal.

"Is there any safe way to carry firearms?" you ask.

My answer, bearing in mind the fact that it is the unexpected which always happens, is *No*. Decidedly and emphatically *No*.

There are, however, some ways which are comparatively safe, or at least, not so dangerous as some others.

I presume the very best method is to carry the gun in both hands, one encircling the grip and the other grasping the fore-end, with the muzzle of the gun elevated at a 45 degree angle. I know of no position from which one can get into action as smoothly and quickly as this. It is only necessary to give the wrist a slight turn outward and the gun butt comes to the shoulder with no other visible effort. It is a posture which I always assume when the dog is on point, but I find it tiresome to carry a gun in that manner all day. Therefore I tuck mine in the hollow of my arm, leaving my left hand free to ward off the twigs which persist in slapping my eyeballs, and to wipe the cobwebs and black spiders from my perspiring face.

Another thing which might well be classed as a useful art is the trick of falling gracefully. No matter if you are as sure-footed as a mountain goat, if you follow a bird dog the time will come when you will embrace Mother Earth. Whether you arise, crestfallen and ashamed, to a chorus of hoots and jeers, or come up smilingly, like a stage star taking a curtain call, is a thing which lies within your power to control.

I used to hunt with a friend who was cat-like in his foot work. He possessed the instinct, so characteristic of the creatures of the wild, to stay on his feet no matter what happened. His singleness of purpose in this regard demanded my approbation. Sometimes he would go a whole season without losing his footing, but when he did decide to go down, he did it with the thoroughness which characterized the death of Old Rover. When Old Rover died, if I recall the details correctly, he died all over. My friend fell that way. No half-hearted sitting down on a brier bush, or a lop-sided falling against a tree. He took his falling seriously and went at it with a vigor I have never seen equaled.

I have seen him hook his toe under a stick which re-fused to move, and disengage it with a backward kick, as he leaped forward to regain the balance which was ever just beyond his superbly best endeavor. Like a sprinter leaving the starter's pistol, he would bound forward in amazing leaps, gathering momentum at each jump and leaning ever more and more toward the inevitable horizontal. I have seen him, in that last soul-stirring moment, go headlong into a pile of brush which but thinly concealed the jagged rocks beneath. I have seen him crawl from the debris, his gun barrel scratched and dented, his hands torn, his face cut and bleeding, looking for all the world like a carousing river driver's idea of the end of a perfect day.

Against my will and better judgment I have laughed until my sides ached and my eyes were dim with mirthful tears, while he stood groaning and glowering at me as he dabbed futilely at his wounds with a salvaged handkerchief.

I have always been a clumsy lout and early learned, for self-preservation, to fall with less of that earth-vibrating jar. It is the simplest of all matters to flex the knees instantly when a foot suddenly refuses to follow its predecessor, and in that instant extend the left hand and touch the ground. If badly off balance, I then roll over on my side, keeping the gun free, and although I average to fall in this manner a dozen times a day, I have never yet had a bruise or scratch to show for it. It is much easier to fall than to try, even successfully, to stay on one's feet.

At all times, and especially while falling, keep the gun pointed at the ambient atmosphere. I have the impression that the stopping of a charge of shot or a rifle ball from the distance of a few feet would not be an enjoyable experience. In support of my theory and to close a not too pleasant chapter, I append the following extract from a letter received recently:

"As you know, Santa-Cruz Island is only a short distance from here. About seventy miles. I know a chap—in fact he lived with me on Seventh Street for a few weeks when he was down and out—who piloted a pleasure yacht from Wilmington Harbor.

"He made frequent trips to Santa-Cruz with boar-hunting parties, and I had a standing invitation to go at any time. I intended to do so but several things prevented, and then a member of a hunting party was shot and Bill gave up the hunting trips.

"The death of the young man was very tragic. No one

ever learned how it happened. He went up a canyon alone. Some minutes later his partner heard a shot, went over, and found him staggering about with his throat shot half away. He never lost consciousness until a few minutes before he died. He was unable to talk but wrote on leaves from a writing tablet. 'Radio Pasadena for Dr. So-and-so.' 'Get him by plane,' etc. Bill showed me the notes. Toward the last they grew more illegible. The last few words nearly covered a blood-stained page. 'Getting weak—loss of blo—,' and that was the finish." — wow

LYNN
BOGUE
HUNT

CHAPTER VIII

WHEN I had the cocksure wisdom of youth I knew exactly what should be done to increase the supply of grouse and woodcock in our coverts, but now that I have rolled up an average mileage on the pathway of life, I am not so egotistical about my wisdom.

Of one thing, however, I am firmly convinced. Back of all the chaos which we call life, beyond the realms of unmeasurable and unfathomable space, in which millions of celestial bodies move with unfailing accuracy, there is some definite and perfect plan. You may call it what you will —coincidence—nature—God. Neither your opinion nor mine can alter a single sequence of it. It is inexorable. When its fitful shadow hovers malignantly close, we shudder at its harshness; and yet it is always just.

No living species can flourish beyond a certain point. A proper balance must be maintained or that species is doomed to extinction. The fact is unalterable—and easily understandable if a moment's thought is given to the matter.

Let us imagine a secluded pond in which are but two varieties of fish—salmon and smelts. So long as a proper proportion of each is maintained, both thrive; but let the limit of that proportion be exceeded by just one fish of either species, and both are doomed to extinction.

Mankind, through its humanity to the weaklings of the race, is building a Frankenstein monster which may eventually destroy it. Nature, through the brutal law of the survival of the fittest, puts ever-new stamina into its children.

That much I know of the law of life. Like every other living creature, grouse and woodcock are governed by that law. They have met changing conditions for ages and have survived. I am optimistic concerning their future. For the past fifteen years their greatest enemy has been the automobile. For a while I was worried concerning the outcome, but they have survived the crucial test and are on the increase once more. Until some other and newer thing menaces them, their future is assured. With plenty of food and shelter, good health, and not too many natural enemies, it is almost unbelievable how plentiful they will become even after a few years of extreme scarcity.

For me there is no greater mystery than the fact that game birds are ever able to rear broods. There are so many enemies which are ever alert to destroy either the eggs or young, that it seems impossible any should survive.

Jim Crow is an old offender. I hate him. I hate his raucous cry, and I dislike the sly and cunning manner in which he flits silently from tree to tree during the nesting season, his bright and peering eyes ever searching for the succulent eggs or young birds in some poorly hidden nest.

[118]

This year I have a special grievance against him. He came to the elm before my house at daybreak one morning this summer and removed from their swinging cradle the entire brood of a pair of Baltimore orioles. He did the job neatly and quickly, getting away before I could possibly get out of doors with my crow exterminator.

I swore vengeance that morning as I watched the stricken parents flying after him and uttering piteous cries. I have not forgotten my vow, and some day this fall I will take toll from that craven raven.

Certain species of snakes eat eggs of birds, and the roaming skunk—as I once heard a farmer remark about his horse—"eats anything he can get his hands on." The occasional mink and the more common weasel prey heavily upon the helpless young and are not averse to slitting the throats of adult birds. The silently floating owl takes toll each day of the year from some of the lesser folk, and the hawks hunt diligently throughout the duration of their stay with us.

My friend "Docwood" advances the interesting theory—which certain incidents I have observed seem to strengthen—that hawks hunt by scent left in the air.

Now "Doc" is a keen student of nature and is not one to jump hastily at a conclusion. I think he is undoubtedly correct. He relates how, while on a fox stand one morning

[119]

in a bit of cleared land between two evergreen forests, he heard a grouse get up some distance away, and saw her fly across the clearing into the woods beyond.

After she had gone from sight a full minute, a large hawk sailed out through the trees and beat across the clearing in the path of the grouse. The two events were not then correlated in Doc's mind, and he dismissed them from his thought.

A minute or two later, however, he heard the grouse flush again, and once more she came across the clearing and into the wood on his side. Shortly afterward the hawk came in sight, questing back and forth in the air in a manner which arrested Doc's attention. The bird seemed to be following the direction taken by the grouse. Again, after another period of time, the grouse came back across the clearing to the thick wood on the other side, and once more the hawk followed, never within sight of his quarry, but ever following accurately its invisible trail. Again the same thing happened; and Doc, the fox forgotten, anxiously awaited the last act of the intense drama. What it was he did not learn, for the grouse came back no more. No sound filtered back through the still, frosty air to hint of the outcome of the tragic event.

It is easy, nevertheless, to visualize the end. The tiring grouse waits a moment too long ere again taking wing, and at last the tireless hawk sights his quarry. With effortless ease he follows the frantic flight of the terrified grouse, drawing ever nearer as her momentum decreases. Her last, despairing plunge to earth in the vain hope of finding a haven. The arrow-like and unerring swoop of the hawk. The spasmodic shuddering of spent wings—and that drama of life is over.

On several occasions, in dense woods, I have flushed a grouse and hawk simultaneously from adjacent trees. I am firmly convinced it was a waiting game, each aware of the other's presence, the grouse hiding in the vain hope the hawk would go away, while he sat patiently awaiting the moment when she should make a betraying movement.

I have seen a hawk swoop at a bird in the act of falling from my gun, and recall with pleasure it was the last act of his wicked life.

I have seen a hawk and rabbit killed with one shot and have known of a hawk and grouse meeting a similar fate.

Reddy Fox takes his toll also, and I am firmly convinced that as difficult as the feat may seem, his toll is not a small one. He is a past master of the cat's method of approach, and he is as swift as lightning in his final spring. Judging from several things I have seen dogs do, and comparing their speed with that of a fox, I feel certain the latter could well catch many grouse throughout the year.

I have seen dogs catch birds which, as far as I have been able to ascertain, were uninjured and in good physical condition just prior to the occurrence.

My first recollection of an incident of this type was in my early hunting days. With a friend and his pointer I went to the seashore looking for plover. With the dog at heel we crept up behind the sand dunes and peered out on the beach before us. It was half-tide, and perhaps fifty yards of hard sand lay between us and the water's edge.

There were no plover in sight, but down where the waves washed the hard-packed sand a flock of twenty or more gulls were clustered around a dead fish.

My friend whispered, "Go get 'em," to the rangy pointer, and he went across that intervening sand at a speed few living things could equal. The birds were engrossed in their feast, and the dog was close by before they saw him. They went into the air simultaneously, with a tremendous beating of wings, and the pointer went up after them. It was a magnificent leap, and, when he came down, he had a gull securely clamped between his capable teeth.

A few years later a young setter of mine caught what appeared to be a perfectly normal grouse. I did not see the thing happen, for the dog was ranging a thicket ahead of me, but suddenly there came the uproar of several grouse rising hurriedly, and a moment later the dog came in with a full-grown one in his mouth. It was a plump, healthy bird and its wings were intact. Just how it happened I would like to know.

Some time later, with another young dog, I saw a grouse lose out in a short and exciting race with him. He had come to a sudden and intense point at the very edge of a small brush-pile in a bit of cut land. There were no trees, but young maples and birches were springing up, here and there, in little clumps not more than three or four feet in height.

I went up to the dog carefully, intending to stroke him and push him a little, for he had a tendency to chase a bird if he got fairly close. I had put my knee against his rump and was in the act of pushing gently against him when a grouse came out of the brush-pile within four feet of his nose. It startled me so much that involuntarily I gave him a decided forward shove, which was all the invitation he needed. He cleared the brush-pile with one mighty leap, and his teeth snapped shut within a foot of the bird's tail. He leaped again and missed by inches. Altitude was the thing the bird needed and, I am sure, desired more than anything else in the world, but it knew, even as I, watching spellbound, knew, the momentary slacking of speed necessitated by that upward surge would be fatal.

The thing did not last more than two seconds, but it

seemed minutes to me. Straight ahead and about three feet from the ground flew the bird, and behind it, his teeth clicking audibly at the termination of each frantic leap, came the dog. At no time after that first leap were they separated by more than two feet, and sometimes by not much more than that many inches.

It was the young maple shoots which decided the matter. The grouse dared not try to rise above them, and occasionally a wing would brush one and slow her up momentarily. Then a half dozen, growing up from an old stump, were directly in her path. I can see it all now as plainly as though it had happened within the hour, the grouse flying with head turned sidewise, charting the course ahead with one eye, and watching the snapping jaws of the dog with the other.

She made her decision instantly and correctly. To swerve around the young shoots would slow her speed a trifle, and there were no trifles to spare. Straight ahead and trust to luck to get through between wing beats was the best bet.

Straight ahead she went, and I thought, for one glorious instant, she would make it, but a wing tip fouled slightly against a springy shoot and swung her the least bit sidewise. It was nothing in itself. The same thing had undoubtedly happened to her thousands of times. In another tenth of a

second she would have righted herself and gone on unharmed, but that moment of time was denied her. The dog
overtook her in mid-air, and this time his snapping teeth
found their mark.

The next fall, in a practically open pasture, I saw that
dog and a fox meet face to face beside a lone, spreading juniper bush. The dog was young and vigorous and believed
that, with an even start, it could outrun any living thing. He
came back several minutes later as disillusioned and crestfallen as any dog it has ever been my fortune to see. This
constitutes one reason why I believe a fox is capable of taking some grouse in his wanderings to and fro upon the
earth.

Occasionally, and thank Heaven it is only at rare intervals, we have an invasion of Arctic owls. When they come it
means but one thing, mighty poor grouse hunting for several years.

If my memory serves me correctly, it was in the fall of
1926 when New England last saw that snowy winged but
black souled ghoul swoop down, on silent pinions, from
the frozen north. Grouse were becoming plentiful once
more, after the unexplained and unprecedented shortage of
1922–1923, and the owls reaped a grim harvest. Not until
the fall of 1930 did they get back to a fair normal.

I speak of the shortage of 1922 as unexplained. It is

more than that. It was almost supernatural. There were an abundance of birds the previous winter. Deer hunters found it almost impossible to stalk their quarry because of the many grouse thundering up ahead of them and warning every wary deer of the hunter's approach.

Trout fishermen found many more than the usual amount of broods that spring. Berry pickers reported grouse everywhere during the summer. Hunters, scouting the coverts, in early September, returned to order extra shells and arrange for additional leave of absence from business. Then, with the opening of the season on October 1st, there were, figuratively, no birds. Literally, there were almost none. In an entire day, in good country and with a good dog, a man might find from two to five single birds. It was not an unusual occurrence to hunt all day without seeing even one.

It was unbelievable. Nowhere did hunters find the tell-tale remains of birds mysteriously stricken with some unknown and deadly malady. It was logical to suppose they had left their accustomed haunts and found refuge in country supposedly unadapted to their needs.

Acting on this theory, bird hunters scouted the swamps, the hilltops, the evergreen thickets and other unlikely places.

It was unthinkable, but true. The grouse were gone. Mysteriously, without leaving any trace, they had vanished in the space of three weeks, and never have I found a man who has been able to tell me how, or where, they went.

Undoubtedly there is some entirely logical explanation, yet, recalling some of the things I have heard—yes—and seen, I wonder.

I may have been ten or twelve years of age when I first heard it. My reason for supposing so is that I was struggling with the old 10 gauge at the time, and wished, mightily, it had been Old Betsy, rather than his expensive, but evidently inefficient 12, which had had the opportunity.

He was a bird hunter and a good one. His character was irreproachable and his name had never been proposed for membership in the Ananias Club. I believed his story implicitly, for those were the Websterian days when I believed anything. Later I came to doubt it and said, with the Psalmist, that all men were liars. Still later I felt, also like the Psalmist, that I had arrived at the conclusion hastily, without giving the matter due thought. Today I believe he told me the exact truth.

He had been hunting, he said, in good grouse country for hours and had not found a single bird. Two days previously they had been plentiful. He could not understand it and, as the afternoon was still young, decided to cross to another covert, which lay beyond an extensive and rather open pasture.

He was halfway across the pasture when, suddenly, the air was filled with flying grouse. They arose as one bird, but in unimaginable numbers. The thing was so unprecedented, so startling, that for a moment he forgot his gun; forgot everything but that swarm of birds before him. Then reason returned, and he let both barrels go into the thickest of the bunch, but the moment of indecision was fatal. The birds were out of range.

"Had I shot when they rose," he said, "I'd have killed a hundred."

"How many were there?" I remember asking.

"A thousand! Five hundred, anyway. The air was brown with them."

"You must have had great shooting on their next rise," I said.

He looked at me solemnly. "That's the part I don't understand, kid," he said. "There wasn't any next rise. I followed them up, expecting to kill the limit in ten minutes, but I didn't find a bird. They just kept on going for whatever place they were headed for. I never saw birds so scarce as they were after that for a year or two."

I think it was in the fall of 1922 or '23 when I again heard a similar story. This time it came from the lips of a hunter luckier than I. He had hunted not only the choicest spots in New England but extensively in the Provinces.

[128]

In all the essential details his story was a replica of the first. He was scouting the unlikely places for birds, motivated by the plausible theory that "if they weren't somewhere, they must be somewhere else." In crossing a high, bald hilltop he had flushed a truly tremendous flock of grouse.

"When I'm in camp," he said, "and hunting stories are governed only by the elasticity of the teller's conscience, I try to keep mine at par, or better, but I am telling the honest, sober truth when I say I believe there were two hundred birds in that flock.

"They got up too far away and went over the crest of the hill. I didn't shoot, but marked their course and went after them, expecting to make history. We put in the remainder of the afternoon, more than two solid hours, looking for them, and the dog never even winded game. Where they went is beyond me."

These were the stories, alike as two peas, yet by no possibility could they have originated from the same source, for distance and time precluded the possibility of these two men having ever met. There was no reason why I should doubt the word of either, yet doubt was present in my mind, even while I wondered why they told such Munchausenlike stories.

I knew how a novice would put up a pair of birds, convince himself that there were four or five in the flock, follow and start them several times more, and leave the wood empty handed, but with the firm conviction he had started at least a score of birds. I knew the tyro's propensity for declaring a flock of ten birds to contain at least fifty, but this hunter painstakingly tallies and records each bird started throughout the season, shrewdly estimating whether a certain bird has or has not been counted on a previous rise. "Why," I asked myself, "should a man of that type estimate a flock of possibly ten birds to contain at least two hundred?"

For several years the question remained unanswered. Then, one memorable afternoon, on my way home, after vowing to hunt no more until the birds were more plentiful, I stumbled into one of those mythical flocks myself.

There were not two hundred birds. There were not even one hundred. But there were more than I ever thought that territory could produce in a bumper year. According to my best judgment there were from forty to fifty birds. They went up simultaneously with a thunderous roar which might have been heard a half mile away. It was disconcerting, but I had been awaiting that opportunity for more than twenty years and had outlined a plan to meet this crisis, should it ever occur.

No flock shooting for mine. I would pick one bird and

make sure of him. I did that. It was the nearer bird, but he was farther than I care to have them. He was hard hit with the first shot and hung almost immovable in mid-air. The second shot brought him down and I stood, with empty gun, while that mighty flock of grouse sailed across the clearing, swung over and across the wide river, and disappeared among the trees on the other side.

There was no way of following them across the river, so I went home and passed a sleepless night as I laid plans for the morrow.

For several days thereafter, I haunted that territory with all the tenacity of Hamlet's ghost. In those succeeding days, if my memory is correct, I found just one bird. The others had vanished; gone, utterly, beyond the ken of mortal man.

I do not understand it. I wish that I might. What age-old instinct is it which causes them to band together thus? Does some heritage from those primordial days when the world was young, still linger within their mottled breasts? Do they still possess some migratory instinct which calls them with a power they cannot withstand? I know this to be true of certain small European animals which, periodically, leave their mountain homes and swarm down to the seacoast in uncountable thousands. Neither wind nor tide nor icy waves can check the mighty urge which draws them on, and they swim, a solid phalanx, into the briny deep, questing, until the end, that forgotten land which, a million years ago, sank to the ocean's floor.

Does some such primal urge still stir, periodically, beneath the crest of the wily grouse? I do not know. But often, on a winter's night, I sit by the fire and ponder. Why those mighty flocks? To where do they disappear? Why the great scarcity afterward, I wish I knew the answer.

Man, the master, takes heavy toll from his friends of the wild, but his season is so restricted that I doubt if he rates as the greatest destructive agency.

Countless birds live a lifetime and die of old age without ever seeing a human being, and in these modern times, too, when the forests are far below their old-time vast proportions.

Despite the fact that he is a born killer, modern man is learning, slowly, the value of game conservation. The wise hunter no longer cleans out a territory, even though the opportunity presents. I have seen the thing done, in the old days, with disastrous results. It was years before those coverts provided even normal shooting, and it was not in a period of extreme scarcity elsewhere, either.

One of my shooting friends keeps a comprehensive census of the numerous coverts he hunts throughout a season. He is capable of making a shrewd estimate of the grouse each section contains, after thoroughly working it with his dog. He not only estimates how many birds are necessary to reseed the covert the ensuing year, but he allows generously for the probable kill of other hunters and allots a generous amount to the killers of the wild. If, at the close of the survey, there are any excess birds, he tries his best to take them. If there are none, he takes not as much as a single grouse from that particular territory.

Woodcock, being a migratory bird, cannot be so easily tabulated. In the flighting season they are, like mortal man, "here today and gone tomorrow." I have noticed one unusual thing in the years I have hunted. That it has been nothing but a happy coincidence makes it not one whit the less appreciated. When grouse are the scarcest, we usually have an abundance of woodcock. I can see no relation of the two facts. There is no more reason for it than for rainy week ends, but the idea meets with my favor, and I am properly grateful.

To me it always seems that wing shooting was more of a sporting proposition than other methods of hunting birds. I do not know that this is so. It is merely my personal viewpoint, and I would cede to every man, but one, the privilege of hunting as he chooses. There is, I am told, a real thrill in hunting with a good tree dog. Lying in wait at certain favored feeding grounds appeals to some, as does the stealthy stalking of birds on the ground. I have no criticism to offer concerning these methods of hunting, or of the deadly fan formation with three and sometimes four men. If you get your greatest enjoyment from any of these methods, or from some carefully worked out system of your own, I am entirely in accord.

But for the man who shoots budding grouse, often out of season and, more often, easing his conscience with the well worn excuse that the birds are injuring his trees, I have no words to express my indignation. There are proper words. Occasionally, at waterfronts, among overworked stevedores, and among river drivers in Northern Maine when the logs persisted in jamming at a certain point, I have heard terse English eminently adapted to my present requirements. But I have never mastered the art. It requires a long apprenticeship, like diamond cutting, and environment has robbed me of the rare gift that otherwise might have been mine.

Nevertheless, I know what I think of that man, and if you think I think as I think you think, you are exactly right.

I am aware that, from various orchardists, a cry will quite likely arise, upon reading this, that will reach to high Heaven. I am almost positive of this fact, because faint echoes of a similar plaint are still ringing in my tortured eardrums.

In a recent magazine article on grouse I said, among many other unimportant things, that the damage done to apple trees was oftentimes overestimated. In fairness to my-self, I beg to state that in the original draft of the article, I conceded the fact that grouse may, with severe budding, seriously distort the shape of very young trees. But, because space was an important factor, I was forced to elide many such observations, and the final draft stated, rather baldly, that the supposed injury to apple trees by budding grouse was just "another fallacy."

That the grouse-loving sportsmen throughout the land appreciated it, a drawer full of congratulatory letters indi-cates, but the orchardists seemed to possess an entirely dif-ferent point of view. To a man, they failed dismally in ap-preciating my humor and spontaneous wit. Mercenary as Croesus, they thought only in terms of apples, and de-scribed me as accurately, with convincing adjectives, as though they had known me for years.

Those words "another fallacy" were ill chosen. Not an orchardist in the country, even though his system could assimilate green apples by the barrel, could digest those two simple words.

A certain New England grower seemed the most fair.

He states, in an extract from one paragraph of his letter: "A grouse will feed at daylight and dusk, two to three hun-

dred buds to a meal (a potential bushel of apples) from November first to April fifteenth."

This statement, among many others, he labels "a few
facts." Now there is an old axiom that facts are stubborn
things. Another trite saying informs us that figures are little
George Washingtons. Therefore, if we combine his stubborn facts and my truthful figures, we should arrive at some
definite and, undoubtedly, interesting conclusions.

The orchardist states that 20 bushels is an average crop
per unbudded tree. Let us, then, suppose he had a block of
166 trees adjacent to a grouse covert where, by some fortui-
tous circumstance, five pairs of grouse were spared. Unbudded, the trees would have yielded exactly 3,320 bushels
of luscious, juicy McIntosh apples, but alas, alack, for 166
days those ten grouse have devoured 20 potential bushels
per day, with the result that my friend, the orchardist, gets
not even one teeny weeny little apple for himself. No, not
even a wormy one. And if, perchance, there were eleven
grouse in that territory, it would have been necessary for
him to go out and borrow 332 bushels (and not "potential"
bushels either) to make up the deficit. He cannot fail to
admit that this is so. He said so, very, very plainly.

I personally know of one apple tree that was budded by
five grouse until the last visible bud was taken. That spring
the tree was given especial care. It was fertilized heavily,

sprayed consistently and, with the coming of fall, bore 14 bushels of choice fruit, which was the largest single crop it ever produced. I do not know the exact number of days those five birds budded that tree, but it was a long time. I am certain that two weeks would be a very conservative estimate.

Still figuring from those incontrovertible "facts," those five grouse destroyed 140 bushels, which, combined with the fourteen that were harvested, would have given to that one tree, if it had remained unbudded, the not insignificant total of 154 bushels; a harvest, that, while perhaps not establishing a record, might still be vulgarly termed a bumper crop.

Nature gives to each tree a score of blossoms for each fruit she expects it to bear. She dries up much of the young fruit and causes it to fall, that certain more favored ones may mature. Man, if he be wise, goes Nature one better and removes much of the remaining crop, that he may harvest better fruit and relieve the tree of some of its enormous task.

Many orchardists claim there is no similarity between the modern cultivated apple tree and the prolific, everbearing, wild tree which withstood the deadly ravages of the savage grouse since the beginning of time, or apple trees, if you require accuracy.

With this statement I most heartily disagree. The modern, pampered and highly cultivated apple tree is still Nature's child. The ruffed grouse is also that, and not one-quarter part the problem to me that are the small boys, and men with youthful characteristics, who year after year harvest my choicest apples, without one penny of expense to me. I prune and fertilize and spray. God, from His largess, gives the increase and, in His infinite wisdom knows, I hope, who gets the apples.

CHAPTER IX

AS I look back, over a greater period of years than I care to count, I am conscious of the fact that I must have been pretty thoroughly interested in bird hunting.

In the old days the open season began September 15th and lasted until December 1st. There was no season limit. One's conscience and his ability to kill birds were the only agents that governed the seasonal kill.

As soon as I attained an age where I could barter my summer services for a fall vacation, I hunted every suitable day throughout the entire season. The unsuitable days were a very rare occurrence. No ordinary rain made the slightest difference. It had to be an equinoctial affair to register in my consciousness. Neither was wind a factor. Many a day I have come out into a clearing that commanded a clear view of the storm tossed Atlantic and seen the horizon dotted with the sails of coastwise craft running, with rails awash, for the nearest port. On the occasional days when both wind and rain combined to make a storm of such Gargantuan proportions that falling trees made woods traverse an actual menace, I hunted ducks and geese.

Ere it slips my memory, may I state that not once did I catch cold from exposure. On hundreds of different occasions I have come in so thoroughly drenched that my skin was white and shrunken.

I have sat for ages in a duck blind, so wet and cold that it was an even gamble whether or not I would ever be able to get on my feet again.

For several winters I made a practice of choosing those days when the tide was low at sundown to hike five miles around a road and across a bridge over a river that separated me from the best duck shooting in our vicinity.

When the evening flight was over, I would leave that eel grass bed, come down the river bank to a point opposite my home, which was now not more than a mile distant, sit down on a convenient ice cake, and divest myself of every rag of clothing. I would make a neat bundle of these, tie them to the gunbarrel, and wade out into that icy salt water. If I had gauged the tide correctly, and the hard sand of the river bed was of its customary smoothness, the water would be of a uniform depth, about halfway from my waist to my armpits. On more than one occasion, however, the salty tang of it has been on my lips when I waded out on the further shore. Undressing, after a brisk half-mile walk, was one thing; dressing again, after that fifty yards of icy brine, was something else again. But that last homeward mile in double quick time, and a genuine old-fashioned New England supper put me absolutely right, and never did one wayward, inadvertent little sneeze warn me that I had done aught else but a perfectly wise and logical thing.

Yet, strange to relate, if, on some balmy summer evening, I step out of doors in my slippers to take a last, ancient Mariner's squint at the weather aloft, before turning in, it will require the combined services of a homeopathic doctor, a chiropractor, and all the herb-brewing old women in the neighborhood, to prevent me from having pneumonia, peritonitis, asthma, lockjaw and muscular rheumatism, with complications.

If one hunted steadily in those days, it required a pretty fair amount of physical stamina. There was no stepping into a car and getting out five minutes later at a covert five miles distant. We walked, by preference through the woods, and when the day was ended, we walked home again.

I wish I knew how many miles I traveled, in those days, for each bird I killed. There is no way of tallying up on it now, but for the past several years I have kept a record of my auto mileage through the hunting season, as well as of the number of birds taken. I find that I drive approximately ten miles for each grouse bagged, and about half that distance per woodcock. It is not necessary, but the far places have always seemed, to me, the fairest. I would much rather drive ten miles to kill one grouse than to bag two in my neighbor's back yard.

I am further convinced I was an exceptionally enthusiastic bird hunter as I recall other incidents. It occurs to me now that I wore my one and only driving horse to a mere skeleton as, day after day, I drove about the surrounding country and showed to the one and only girl every last, solitary grouse and woodcock covert that I had located with ten years of arduous toil.

As ludicrous as it must have been, it was, however, a proof of my sincerest devotion, for to no other person upon the earth would I have revealed those storehouses of Nature, laden with a treasure far greater than gold.

Since I first began dragging that old back breaking and shoulder dislocating ten gauge around, until the present time, has been a far cry. Those first years were happy ones, but my one track mind made the periods between hunting seasons seem ages long. With the latter years I have learned to diversify my interests, and have acquired numerous other hobbies, each having its place in relation to the season of the year. I find it a happy solution for the utmost enjoyment of life. Winter sports are forgotten with the coming of spring fishing. With my fly rod and a bit of open water, I am utterly content. With the coming of summer my tackle is forgotten in the ecstatic joy of labor in my gladiolus garden. Hybridizing, listing the new varieties, watching the world's best creations flaunting their loveliness to the crimson east.

Then, as much as I love them, I dig the bulbs two weeks before I should, that nothing may mar my enjoyment of every available day of the grouse and woodcock season.

To have many hobbies is to know contentment. To refrain from boring others with them is a hardship, but it is an absolute necessity if you wish to maintain friendly companionship with your everyday associates.

To me, it always seemed a bit nauseating when a man, or woman, showed unmistakable evidence of inflation beneath the hatband. No man is quicker to applaud genius than I, or to give credit where it is due, but I like to see it accepted with becoming modesty.

The genius has no justifiable reason for egotism for he was born with brains. The plodder, who makes good in a certain line of endeavor, has done nothing any other man, of average mentality, could not have done, had he so chosen.

Why, then, should a sportsman, of only average ability, become so imbued with a sense of his God-given superiority that he is unbearable? The only amusing thing in hunting with men of this type is their frequent and amazing stock of alibis. If they score a hit, it is a shot that Annie Oakley, in her palmy days, could not have equaled. If they miss, as they do with convincing regularity, it is always some untoward incident, over which they had no control, which caused it.

[143]

"The bird turned, just as I pulled the trigger," they will say. To be sure she did. That was a direct result of her college education. Yet a moment before, and a moment after, she was flying a straight course.

"I was holding absolutely right on her but that d——n tree got in the way." Or, "I'll bet I don't use this brand of ammunition next year. Why, I was centering that bird and got just one measly little feather out of her." "I hit him and I hit him hard, but he didn't come down. That makes eight I've really killed today, and not one single bird to show for it." "If I had the old gun, I'd show you fellows something. Say! I never used to miss a bird with that gun."

One of the most amusing alibis I ever heard was that of a self-styled rabbit assassinator. He was pointing at fresh rabbit tracks in the newly fallen snow. All around the tracks, and for several inches above them in the low alders, were the marks of myriad shot from his gun.

"It doesn't seem possible," he was explaining, volubly, "that a rabbit could get through that pattern. Look at it! There's his tracks and there's the shot marks. There isn't a square inch that hasn't a shot mark in it."

It was true. Absolutely and undeniably true. It was also true that the rabbit was three long and healthy jumps ahead of that particular spot when the shot reached it. I know it to be true, for I saw it with my own eyes.

Personally, I find it much simpler to say, "Chalk down another miss for me. If I can do that just once more it will give me the limit." It is less wearing on my companion's good nature and leaves me in a better frame of mind. I can go after the next one fast and sure.

Some years ago I hunted with a man, on two different days, who must have been a disciple of Coué. With the rising of the sun, he began that never ending, and fearfully tiresome, chant: "Every day, in every way, I'm getting better and better." It is an enviable frame of mind, and I would give much if this power of self-hypnosis were mine. The one weakness in his paean of rejoicing lay in the fact that his comparisons lay not with what he was yesterday, but with what others were at the present moment. Egotism oozed from his every pore, like sugar from an overripe fig.

Not the least of his fabulous accomplishments, as reported to me, was his wing shooting. His praises had been sung to me by a mutual acquaintance and I had come, through their frequent repetition, to believe them.

From early youth it has been my policy to kneel at the feet of wisdom, that I may learn, by emulation, to achieve some small measure of their greatness. Accordingly, I issued an invitation, with all the 'umbleness of Uriah Heep, to share my dog and pet coverts for a day's hunt.

He came, on the appointed day, in a Pullman section,

clothed in English tweeds and high boots, while on his leo-
nine head reposed one of those double barreled hats so in-
timately associated with my mental picture of Sherlock
Holmes. I could assimilate the tweeds and the boots, but
the hat was a hard pill to swallow. I remember wondering
just how the grouse would react to it. Whether an uncontrollable terror would grip them, causing them to fly fren-
ziedly and far, or whether it would excite them to a point
where they would become impolitely curious, was problematical. A suspicion of doubt as to the 24 carat quality of
this bird hunter entered my mind with my first view of that
hat.

When he slid his gun from the sole-leather case I had
other doubts. The gun was a good one but it had acquired
age without polish. No telltale worn checkering here; no
silvered spots on the barrels, which eager hands had grasped
through many glorious autumn days. The only marks of
wear were those acquired in its years in a case. Again a
shadow of doubt crossed my mind.

Less than an hour later, all doubt left my mind forever.
There was no longer any occasion to wonder as to his ability. I knew.

With the dog as immovable as the Rock of Gibraltar, he
walked, unheedingly, past him and nearly went over backward in surprise when a grouse thundered up.

It made a circular flight, peering intently at that comic-strip hat the while, then, its curiosity satisfied, it sailed off about its business, and not until it had traveled seventy-five yards, on the latter course, did that hunter recover sufficiently from his surprise to shoot.

We were in glorious country and he was my invited guest. I'll wager he had more good shots at grouse that day than ever before in his eventful life, and he registered not one hit.

With his first fiasco, I vowed that, come what might, I would not shoot during the day, but would do everything possible to drive birds to him. We left the woods empty handed—a condition which he could not understand—for this was the first time he had failed to bag each bird he shot at.

We said farewell at the home of the mutual friend, and I marked that day, on the calendar, as utterly and irrevocably lost. The next day the mutual friend accosted me.

"What's the matter with you?" he asked, grinning. "Kinda showed you up yesterday, didn't he?"

I inquired why that statement.

"Why, Perce said he took every shot away from you for the whole day. Was that correct?"

"I didn't shoot," I confessed.

"Haw—haw—haw!" Strange that I had never before

noticed how nerve-disturbing was that horselaugh of his. "Haw—haw—haw! Quite a hunter, Perce is, I guess."

"Quite," I agreed. "I wish I might go with him again sometime."

"Haw—haw—haw!" What a raucous sound! "Think you might learn something, huh? I'll tell him. When do you want him to come down?"

"Tell him to come at any time. Tell him I mean it," I urged. "Tell him there isn't another person in the wide world with whom I am so anxious to hunt."

He came, a few days later, in all his erstwhile splendor. We went into the woods together and, this time, I walked by his side. I never saw birds lie better for a dog, or break better for a hunter, than they did on that morning. The gods were kind to me and in exactly fifty-five minutes from the time the dog made his first point, I had taken my limit of six grouse, without missing a shot. Our opportunities had been the same, but he had not discharged his gun.

"I can't take any more today, so I'll play dog for you," I told him, with elaborate politeness.

While there was yet two hours of daylight he shot his last shell. The only casualty was one broken winged grouse. His wailing lament was music in my ears, and I rejoiced in the fact his gun was a larger bore than mine. The thing was a farce, and I was glad it was forever over.

It was a humiliating experience for him, but I felt it was the thing he needed. Perhaps his colossal egotism would know a beneficial shrinkage and his sadly overworked "I's" gain a much needed rest.

One by one I stuffed five grouse in the unstained pocket of his expensive coat, that he might, for once, know the satisfaction of going home with the limit.

He was voluble in his thanks, and my heart knew a certain softening toward him. We said good bye at the crossroads, and I almost experienced a pang of regret at the parting.

The next day I again met the mutual friend. He began that fiendish laughter with his first glimpse of me. Strange that sounds of merriment could be so irritating.

"Haw—haw—haw!" And I used to like the fellow. "Six to one, eh? Pretty one-sided. He told me about it last night. I knew he was good, but I didn't think he could show you up like that. Six to one! He said he took 'em right from under your nose. Oh! Haw—haw—haw!"

There was no sense in trying to explain or to brand him for the miserable, ungrateful liar that he was. I would not be believed and I knew it. I nodded in acquiescence and walked sadly away.

A certain measure of confidence is helpful. Theoretically, if I have mastered a thing and know I can do it with a fair degree of regularity, I should be immune to any nervous attack while doing that particular thing. But it is surprising how doubt will creep in, and it is equally surprising what havoc it can accomplish in a short space of time.

Several years ago I was pheasant hunting and had taken a heavy 12 gauge with 30 inch barrels. I knew I could kill pheasant with it at forty yards, and I was sure of my ability to hold it on anything in the open, for I had used it on ducks.

We found few pheasants that day, but in the afternoon we discovered a new and wonderful grouse country. The underbrush was thick, and I wondered, after missing the first bird to get up, if I could really use that long, heavy gun on grouse. With the second miss I began to believe it might not be possible. Then a pair got up together, an excellent and easy double, but I missed them both. The fifth bird was a perfect open shot. I tried to steady that long barrel on her and make the shot absolutely sure, but the muzzle weight carried me past her, and when I had it steadied at last, I realized the bird was too far away for even a chance shot.

Then I stopped and analyzed the situation. "You," I said to the rattled me, "are capable of killing a grouse occasionally. You know it, so don't worry. Shoot the gun instinctively, without looking at it, and you'll not be far wrong."

The thing seemed logical, and the other me believed it implicitly. I shot at four more grouse that afternoon and killed them as cleanly as I ever did in my life.

I did not become accustomed to the added weight of the weapon in that length of time. Neither was I one whit better marksman than I was a few minutes before. But my confidence was restored by that intimate talk with the inner me, and I was able, once more, to use what little ability I had.

Lack of confidence is a serious handicap. Overconfidence is equally bad. I saw both exemplified at an all day prize shoot in a little Northern Maine town one Thanksgiving Day. I also saw a man with the right proportion of confidence mixed with his genuine ability, and it is needless to say he carried off the money.

I recall the details of that shoot frequently, especially when some nimble-tongued Nimrod, whose ammunition purchases never exceed one box of cartridges per season, starts boasting of the things he can do with a rifle.

The event was held in the little town of Stratton away up in the Dead River region. It was a terminal for deer hunters, and they were there from everywhere. Scores of guides from outlying sporting camps were present, and the gathering represented the best shots from a territory where good shooting was not uncommon.

On that day I saw good shots become unnerved and make unbelievably poor scores through lack of confidence. I saw a pompous individual who had a tremendously exaggerated opinion of his own importance, rudely force his way in ahead of a dozen gentlemen waiting to register. Time was an important factor, he assured us. It was imperative that he catch the afternoon stage out. He must be in New York by morning.

They oiled the way for him, and he shot almost immediately. The butts were six feet square. The targets were twenty-four inches square. The bull was a four inch circle, and the distance one hundred yards.

He shot confidently, with swelling chest, but he shot much too fast. When he had finished the round, he demanded an immediate accounting of his score. I hope I may never forget those succeeding moments. They were the highlights of the day. The attendant came out from his barricade and surveyed the target briefly. Then he elaborately scanned the six foot background, got down on his knees and felt the supporting posts, then patted the ground with questing fingers. At last he stood up and faced the impatient shooter. "It's all right, Captain," he called, in that delightful North Woods drawl. "You didn't hit anything down this way." Amid a long, loud, reverberating roar, the stranger departed hastily for New York.

I saw, on that afternoon, a reserved and capable looking young man shoot the winning score. With his first shot a hush fell over the gathering. There was something in his manner that demanded attention, yet he was, apparently, unaware of the fact. I am sure that ere he raised his rifle for that first shot, the fact that there was a crowd present had passed from his consciousness. He had a job to do and he went about it in a businesslike manner.

The rifle was a Steven's Favorite. He ran a swab through it, reloaded, and unhurriedly released his second shot. That gun-swabbing was a canny trick and precluded the possibility of hurrying.

His final score was 7 in the black and 3 in the first ring, a total of 97 out of a possible 100. It was much the best score of the day, and there were many good men shooting. There was nothing phenomenal about it. Undoubtedly there are many who can beat it. But when a man whose only practice consists in firing a half dozen test shots with the opening of the deer season, tells me he can "hit 'em in the eye every time at two hundred yards," I unconsciously think of that November day when old Mount Bigelow echoed back many thousands of shots which were far from being bull's eyes, or deer eyes, either.

Quite often that man is sincere in the belief that he is entitled to wear the champion's crown, but a few hundred rounds at a target large enough to collect his wildest shots would, or should, convince him of his true worth.

Many a man has said to me, and sincerely too, "I can't shoot at a target, but put game before me and I don't miss very often." Now he may be right, but to me it always seems illogical. If I wished to place the largest number of shots in the smallest possible space, I would go, alone, to some isolated spot and there, carefully and calmly, I would squeeze the trigger when my reason told me my sight was absolutely correct. I am firmly convinced I could do infinitely better work than it would be possible for me to do in the stress of excitement, which rapidly disappearing game always arouses in me.

There are men whose pulse never accelerates a single beat at the things which set my heart thumping like an electric vibrator. There are others who react to excitement and are superb at such moments. Both types are undoubtedly able to shoot as well at game as at an inanimate object, but if I am to believe they can do better, they must furnish convincing proof.

I once saw a really good deer hunter and an all 'round good shot lose money on a wager that he could hit the bigness of a deer three times out of five at a distance of two hundred yards. He had killed deer at that, and greater, distances, but in his narration of the numerous episodes, he forgot to mention the few he had missed at slightly shorter distances.

At last it got under the skin of a friend of mine who was an especially fine rifle and revolver shot. He went into action immediately.

"I'll bet you ten dollars you can't hit the likeness of an average sized deer three times out of five at two hundred yards," he said, and reached for his billfold.

The bet was covered instantly. A committee was appointed at once, and a deer whose measurements satisfied both parties was constructed within the hour. It was transported, by a continuously augmented throng, to the spot selected for the test. On measuring the range the committee found one hundred and seventy-five yards the ultimate distance that could be attained.

"I'll concede the twenty-five yards," said my friend. "Make it one hundred and seventy-five."

"What constitutes a hit?" the rules committee wished to know. "Must the shot be 'fatal' to count?"

"Hoof, horns, or hide," the challenger answered. "If it scratches paint it's a hit."

The first shot was low. I saw the dirt fly between the legs of the target. The second was higher but not quite high enough. The third was far too high. The last two found their mark, one a perfect heart shot, the other about midway of the body. It was poor shooting, not nearly as good as the man was capable of, but it emphasized the fact that occasionally, at two hundred yards, a bullet will wander a bit afield from the groove cut by its predecessor.

That paragraph recalls a letter from a gentleman at one time president of the New Brunswick guides' association. Next to writing of a wounded animal charging the hunter, there was nothing so irritating to him as the custom, practiced by some authors of hunting stories, of naming their shots. I believe I can quote him accurately from memory.

"For G—'s sake," he wrote, "get after the man who writes this sort of stuff: '*My first shot struck him in the thigh and slewed him around; my second shot hit him low down in the brisket; my third split his ear; my fourth struck his right front forefoot; my fifth was a perfect heart shot; etc., etc.*' How in h—l did he know which shot was which? There he is, shooting all over the beast, doing rotten shooting, yet naming each shot like an expert pool player."

Realizing that the foregoing is no feathers off our grouse, I still beg the privilege of quoting one other extract from his letter. It is this:

"I have killed more than fifty bull moose and have lost all count of the number of bears that have fallen to my gun; yet I have never seen or have I known one authentic case where a wounded animal charged the hunter."

[156]

With the little detour completed, I will endeavor to follow along sedately behind Old Duke once more.

This matter of confidence is a sort of round robin affair and has neither a logical beginning nor end. Confidence, in any line, tends to successful effort, and successful effort breeds confidence. Which comes first is as problematical as the old question concerning the bird and the egg, but I am confident a long and patient apprenticeship is necessary before either is permanently attained.

Nerves are fickle masters and I find, in shooting, the better I control mine, the better is my score. For me, it is absolutely essential to live one moment at a time; the past, with its failures, forgotten; the future, with its possibilities, undreamed of.

Long ago I learned, in trap shooting, to take each target as it came and forget all else. To think of a lost bird was disastrous. To think that another twenty straight would give me a perfect score was equally fatal. If I had that serene sureness of ability, and thought only of the target about to be sprung, I shot my best possible score.

In bird hunting, I have learned to try a hundred different devices to ease the nervous tension and have found that carrying another thought in the mind, in addition to the primal one of killing game, is a distinct advantage.

Interest in the work the dog is doing; laying a bet with

[157]

yourself as to which way the bird will go; gambling you can get her within a prescribed distance; any foolish device with which you can momentarily delude yourself into believing the actual hitting of the bird to be a secondary consideration, will suffice.

My greatest nerve panacea is in trying to outguess the bird. With each step the panorama changes before one. A lane that would afford a perfectly clear shot becomes an impenetrable thicket when one has moved a few steps ahead. The perpetual riddle as to just where the bird is and the course it will take is not unsolvable. Thrashing about promiscuously when the dog is pointing, and trusting to luck for a shot when the bird gets up, has never been my idea of deriving the utmost enjoyment from the sport. The man who hunts year after year and does not learn something of the habits of his quarry is a mighty poor scholar; yet I have hunted with men who have been too surprised to shoot when a grouse chose to fly in a direction anyone might have known she would take. The position of the dog in relation to the hunters, the topography of the ground, and the direction of the wind had determined that factor long seconds before she took off.

More than any bird I know, a grouse dislikes to fly. Undisturbed, it will stay on the ground day after day with no thought of taking wing, and when it does start, it has already picked its course on the map. The occasional bird which is not aware of your approach until you are about to step on him is the exception to the rule. What he will do is as unknown to him as to you, but you may be assured he will do it quickly. If you stop him, you must be on the job instantly. There is a noticeable difference in the speed of grouse. Some thunder upward with a startling amount of noise and seem to make little headway, while others slip away with the speed of an arrow and with little more noise.

Several years ago it came to my attention, after a period of days in which a strong wind blew, that the majority of grouse started during that time flew against the wind. That aroused my interest and, for several years thereafter, I kept a record of the flight of one hundred birds. I have become convinced that they do, by preference, rise against the wind. It is far from necessary for them to do it, for they can slide off a stump or log, or from good old Mother Earth, and go down wind as smoothly as anything extant, but my figures show that approximately seventy out of each hundred have got up into the wind. Last year I hunted with that theory present in my mind, and it led to some very interesting moments and brought several birds to bag which I would not have taken a year or two previously.

The game of bird hunting has always been more enjoyable to me when I have had a good companion with whom to hunt. Choosing a partner is a momentous question, as every married man with solemn hand upraised toward Heaven, will testify. The matter of choosing a shooting companion requires no less deliberation.

My partner must have a mind of his own. He must be capable of reasoning out for himself matters relating to the sport and must have the courage to stand for his convictions. No "yes, yes" man for mine; I am so often wrong, but so eternally anxious to know the right, that I cannot tolerate the man who always agrees with me.

He must be broad-minded enough, however, to play the game on a 50-50 basis, respecting my expressed wishes as I respect his.

If we are hunting with his dog, I must never criticize any fault in it, and I must be quick to notice and praise any particularly fine work he does. If he is hunting with me, I must refrain from asking him what he thinks of the work of my dog. If he knows it to be good, he will mention the fact. If it is but ordinary, I should not endanger the chances of his soul's salvation by making him lie and say it is superb.

The man I ask to hunt regularly with me must be cool and collected in moments of stress. He must consider my safety first and shoot at no bird that flies in my direction. He must have a sense of humor, a controllable temper, and possess the ability to take a joke without harboring malice.

For years I stole shots from a companion with whom I have hunted more than with any other man in the world. I had been blessed with some years of experience before he took up the game, and consequently my speed was in excess of his. He had, it seemed to me, the ability to make a mighty fine bird hunter, and because I liked him and wished to speed up his shooting, I used, quite often, to kill a bird on which he was swinging.

Never did I fail to apologize, with grave face and humble manner, pleading as an excuse for my unpardonable breach of etiquette, the fact that I thought, from his leisurely swing, he was not in a position to see the bird.

The thing went on for a year or two and then, one fall, I found, when I tried the trick, I merely doubled with him, both shots exploding simultaneously and sounding as one. He had attained the desirable speed and I dropped the practice of that trick immediately, but he had not forgotten. Before the season was ended I learned, more than once to my chagrin, that any easy target at which I took a leisurely swing was as likely to find its way into his pocket as mine.

He still does it, and never apologizes. It is not necessary for him to do so. He just looks over and grins, and I, knowing he is thinking of the old days, grin cheerfully back.

I know of no more pleasant relationship than this. Our

methods of hunting are identical. When the dog gives us a point, I know by a swift topographical survey exactly what my friend will do. It is not necessary to speak. I can carry out my part of the campaign and know he will properly execute his. If that bird lies for the dog, for only a few seconds, it is pretty certain he will be saluted when he leaves. I need not worry if the bird comes my way; no charge of shot from my friend's gun will penetrate my shrinking flesh. I can concentrate on killing the bird and, if I fall down on the job, no word of reproach will grate on my sensitive nerves. He may state, emphatically, that it might be wise to consult an oculist, but I know he is "kidding" me and I await with pleasure the moment when I can offer to lend him my glasses.

During lunch, or on the way to and from the shooting grounds, we may argue, sometimes heatedly, on diversified matters, yet part, at the close of the day, with a friendly "good night."

I recently received a letter from a business man who is blessed with much of this world's goods. His passion for good dogs and guns can be gratified to the point of satiation. He can, and does, take the time to hunt when and where he chooses, and he is an excellent shot.

Yet, with all his advantages, he writes that he is extremely unhappy. In his wide circle of acquaintances he has found not one kindred spirit whom he may choose for a hunting companion.

I envy him not. I like him immensely and, because of that, wish he might partake of the riches that are mine.

One of my keenest joys is derived from taking a bright and likeable young boy into the woods. I do not know whether it is the lingering effect of those glorious days with Dad which have softened my spirit, or whether I have, happily, not outgrown my boyish characteristics, but I do know that I enjoy it immensely. There is no animation like that on the face of a boy when he sees a dead grouse come crashing down through the tree tops; no gaze so reverent as that which he bestows on my worn old gun. Most often it is that old weapon which he places on the pedestal. I am nothing; the dog is nothing; the gun is the embodiment of all his dreams of prestige and power. He is convinced that, with a weapon such as mine, he could stop anything which moves upon, or over, the earth. I do not disillusion him for I hope, some day, he may own and cherish one as good.

I recall one occasion when we were hunting a covert far from home. It was good grouse country and we were familiar with it, for distance has never kept me from hunting good territory. We had just bagged our first bird when I heard footsteps approaching and, looking back, saw a pair of bright faced boys coming, apologetically, toward us.

It did not require much encouragement to elicit the fact they had never seen a bird dog work. An invitation to follow along and enjoy that pleasurable experience was accepted gratefully. The gods were kind to those boys that day. Never did a dog do better work, and we took six grouse from the covert in short order. When we had finished our hunting there, we came back to the car and prepared to drive to another interesting shooting ground a few miles farther on.

We were ready to depart when one of the boys mustered sufficient courage to ask if we had ever hunted a certain birch covered knoll, which he pointed out with a shapely, sun browned hand. I told him we had not. It did not look like grouse country to me. Too far from heavy timber and too sparsely wooded.

But the boys insisted there were "pa'tridge" on the knoll.

Quite certain in our minds that it was but a subterfuge on their part to spend another hour in our illustrious company, we went nevertheless. We hunted less than ten minutes and bagged the four birds necessary to complete our limit, I with a clean double, and my partner with two snappy singles.

Never have I seen eyes protrude farther than did the startled orbs of those two boys. They went into a huddle.

Listening carefully, I caught part of the conversation. ". . . said he'd give me a bicycle for my birthday; . . . rather have a dog" ". . . my father's gun."

We bade them good bye with real regret. They were bird hunters in the making, and the future held much in store for them. Unfortunately I have not seen them since that day, but—well, here's hoping they break nicely for you this fall, fellows.

Bird hunting is a serious business, yet, when we reflect on the frailties of human nature, it is humorous to think that a sane business man will forsake his means of livelihood for a week or more, drive any distance up to five hundred miles, buy a nonresident license, chase a bird dog up hill and down dale for a period of days through storm and shine, will swelter, sweat, and swear, yet if he is so fortunate as to bag a half dozen grouse, will drive the long way home with sparkling eyes and glowing cheeks, vowing that he has had the happiest experience of his life.

I pride myself that with the passing years I have come to know a reasonable amount of sanity in relation to grouse hunting. If it rains hard enough to drench me to the hide while going from the house to the garage, I can, by exercising my will power, convince myself that the day is not the best one for tramping through the brush behind a dog.

Likewise, if it is so cold that the car, after an exhaustive session with starter and hand crank, refuses to do more than cough occasionally and asthmatically, I am now able to wait a half hour for the weather to moderate somewhat.

I have lost much of the fierce impetuosity of youth, and physical comfort counts for more than it did once. Witness the following:

A few years ago I met with a minor accident just prior to the opening of the bird hunting season. I came through without a scratch, with the exception of my left foot, in which a small bone was broken. It was very painful, so much so, in fact, that I could not attend to business.

Now I have always held to the theory that there is health and life giving properties in fresh air and sunshine, in the soft pungent odor of pine and the spicy tang of balsam fir. Therefore it seemed reasonable to suppose what was good for the body would likewise be good for my injured foot. Accordingly I proceeded to put my theory into practice, and hobbled out forthwith, a shotgun under my arm, and an eager dog calling me on and on.

It was exactly the treatment I needed. There was a decided improvement in my condition within thirty days, and at the end of the season I was entirely cured.

Had I carried a movie camera that fall, I might have

taken a film that would have ranked with the masterpieces of the art. Charlie Chaplin, in his palmy days, might have conceived the thought. He might also have played the major role in the piece, but he never could have achieved the consummate artistry of the unheralded and unsung Thespian who enacted it for me alone.

Gene and I were hunting one of our best loved coverts, up near Lake Winnepesaukee in New Hampshire. It was one of the largest and most interesting bits of bird country in our whole list, and also the hardest to hunt. An unusual phenomenon is noticeable from the moment you step out behind the dog. Travel in any direction you choose, North, East, South or West, going in or coming out, every step of the way is uphill. One walks, with aching knees and lifeless feet, buoyed up by the hope that level land lies just beyond the scope of his vision, but it never does. To make a bad matter worse, the earth is strewn with sharp edged rocks that make each step a hazard.

But it is wonderful grouse country. There are innumerable alder thickets and tiny brooks, the latter all defying the law of gravity and running uphill, and the surrounding mountains are covered with heavy timber which affords ample and adequate winter protection for thousands of grouse.

It was mid-afternoon, and we were on the way out, with

nearly the limit of birds. I was hobbling along some fifty yards from Gene, and Count was quartering the ground before us. He came over toward me, slowed up, went on a few careful steps, and pointed quite intensely at the base of a low branching evergreen tree.

I worked in cautiously, momentarily expecting a grouse to go up, but whatever it was, it was lying close. With gun ready, I circled the tree, and there, standing sedately on the sunny side, was a gaunt old sheep. They were not uncommon in that territory, in fact, we had seen a big flock in the lowlands that day, but it was unusual to see one alone. Something in her dejected attitude drew my attention, and I approached to see if she were afraid. I was almost within reaching distance of her when she jumped awkwardly away, and then I saw what was the matter. A massive, double spring fox trap was solidly clamped to her right forefoot, and to the trap was attached a three foot chain and a dragging block of wood.

Here was a dumb animal in distress, and my sympathy was at once aroused.

Cautiously I approached, thinking I could get close enough to grasp her by a quick movement, but at the last instant she eluded me. I tried again with the same result. Then I called Gene. He came over and I explained the situation.

"I can't catch her with this bum foot," I said, "but perhaps I can head her off so you can get hold of her."

"When I need any help to catch a sheep with a trap and grapple that size fastened to her, I'll ask for it," he boasted. With that he leaned his hundred dollar Winchester against a low spruce, spat on his hands, and went into action.

His first efforts were patterned after my method of approach and were equally unsuccessful, whereupon he resorted to subterfuge and walked as though he intended to pass her at a distance of several feet. She stood quietly watching him, and when he was exactly opposite her, he turned and sprang, leopard-like, for her. At the psychological moment, just as his hands were about to grasp her abundant fleece, she made one quick jump ahead. Gene's groping hands grasped nothing more substantial than the atmosphere, and his momentum carried him twenty feet downhill.

He turned, shedding his shooting coat as he came. It was unseasonably warm, but I had a suspicion that not the sun alone was responsible for the ruddy glow on his face.

This time he went after her like a hawk after a sparrow, with a singleness of purpose which was praiseworthy. But the old ewe seemed to divine his intention, for she started off at a lumbering gallop, the unwieldy trap and clog threatening, momentarily, to throw her. Gene sprinted

[169]

over the rock-strewn ground and rapidly cut down the distance which separated them. In his younger days he was a football player of no mean ability and now, as he closed in on the fleeing animal, I envisaged him once more tearing across the gridiron, as in the old days, grim and remorseless as fate.

To further carry out the illusion, he launched himself, while yet a few feet distant, in a perfect flying tackle. It was superbly executed and reflected credit on his old coach. It would have been eminently successful had it not been for an unforeseen incident which, while not detracting one whit from the flawless beauty of the tackle, robbed it of much of its effectiveness.

In that instant when the flying form hovered above her, the sheep planted all four feet stiffly and stopped as suddenly as though she had collided with a brick wall. Gene, however, went on and on, like a straying comet, in an elongated parabola that was a geometrical joy. He came down, principally upon his face, ricocheted from rock to rock, and came at last to a skidding halt. The sheep stood regarding him gravely for a moment and then said, "Baa-a-a," with an intonation I hope I may never forget.

Until that moment the play had been logical and commonplace; nothing about the scenery or actors had suggested that this was to be anything but a homely little drama. But with that derisive "Baa-a-a," the piece was wafted to a loftier plane and became, at once, a glorified, yea, an immortal burlesque.

Thinking that the dog might possibly aid us, I blew my whistle, whereupon Gene rolled over and got shakily up on one knee. He muttered something about not taking him out of the game and assured an imaginary someone he would be all right in a minute. With that he got to his feet, leaned over, placed his palms on his knees, and glared wildly about.

His gaze at last encountering the questioning eyes of the sheep, he stared fixedly at her and reason slowly returned. He grinned, straightened up, and went after her again.

I am sure nothing more ludicrous ever happened. He, running after that elusive animal until his breath was spent; I, hobbling, like a peg-legged sailor, in a vain attempt to head her toward him, while the dog brought up the rear, walking as stiff legged as though on stilts, pointing exactly as he did on a running grouse.

How long it lasted I have not the slightest idea. I recall Gene sitting down several times while he gasped for oxygen with all the fervor of a netted fish. In those all too infrequent intervals I also gasped for breath and held my aching sides.

[171]

It ended, alas, all too soon. Actuated by what reason, or lack of it, I know not, the old ewe stopped suddenly, and moved not so much as an eyelash while Gene staggered up and threw both arms around her neck for support. It was too much for her, in her weakened condition, and they went down together, amalgamated, in a lifeless heap. Foot after leaden foot I approached, until I could reach down and grasp the chain in a grip that nothing but death could loosen, whereupon I added my form to the recumbent heap. With that, Count, observing that we had at last bagged our game, decided it was no longer necessary to continue pointing, and came in and lay down beside us.

When strength had returned, we sat up and, after a time, removed the trap. Getting laboriously to our feet, we started back over the tortuous way we had come and, after a moment, the sheep uttered a plaintive "Baa-a" and followed us.

"Everywhere that Mary went—" quoted Gene. "Have you any idea where I left that d—n gun?"

I had an idea, but it proved to be wrong. We had gone far, by a circuitous route. To retrace our steps was an impossibility. There seemed to be nothing to do but to trust to luck and hope that darkness would not come too soon.

"If I lose that gun," said Gene, "I might just as well give up bird hunting. I wouldn't take a thousand dollars for it!"

"It should be easy to find," I said. "You stood it up against a small hemlock, or spruce, or fir."

"That simplifies matters a h—l of a lot, doesn't it? All we need do is look under every soft-wood tree in this forty thousand acres—*look at that dog, will you?*"

Count was straightened out on a magnificent point. I circled him and put up the bird, but she chose to rise behind an evergreen and was hidden from my sight. To Gene she presented a perfect cross shot, while he stood, impotently, and watched her out of sight. His remarks were brief but very appropriate, and in the midst of them the sheep, which still lingered a few feet behind us, uttered another derisive "Baa-a."

He turned and poured a flood of invective on her so sulphurous in its nature that I expected to see the fleece seared from her emaciated frame. I gathered from his remarks it was quite unlikely he would ever take up sheep farming in a serious way.

We found the shooting coat first, and then it was a simple matter to locate the gun. He fell on it like the father upon the neck of the prodigal son, petted and polished it, worked the action fondly, and slid it under his arm with a sigh of great content. Then, as the day was far spent, we started down the heartbreaking, uphill trail toward home.

[173]

I have spoken oft of Count. I have said, many times, he was the best grouse dog I have ever seen. He has gone now to limitless coverts, and his soft brown eyes no longer prejudice me in his favor. I have had time to reflect soberly upon those virtues and faults which were his, and again I reiterate:

He was the finest grouse dog it has been my fortune to know.

My affection for him was sincere. I am sure he realized this and, as best he could, he returned it. His love, however, centered upon one man, his owner and my friend. He would go out of his way to greet me, and show by every possible artifice he liked me, but his eyes were always upon his master. In the woods he seemed to recognize the fact that I was an important factor. He hunted impartially and gave me my share of the favors, but never, but once, did he drop a dead bird at my feet. That gesture constituted the strongest evidence I have found that animals do possess reasoning powers. I have heard far smarter men than I argue that they do not, with logic that was indisputable, but, well, here's the story.

It was the first day of the first year of open season on pheasants in New Hampshire. We were hunting grouse, and, in a sparsely wooded pasture between two old orchards, Count began roading a running bird. It traveled far, but at last he pointed staunchly, close to an old wall, and we knew the bird was lying close. We went in cautiously and were well up to the dog when a cock pheasant got up with a raucous cackle and thundering wings. He presented me with a perfect shot, straightaway and rising sharply, and I gave him the right barrel. He was hard hit, but he stayed afloat and banked sharply to the right. Centering him again, I gave him the works once more. With the impact of the shot he swung around, and setting his wings, planed off in a long and gradual descent.

Count had been watching proceedings with a great deal of interest, and now, at the order to fetch, he started off, willingly enough, but with little of his customary enthusiasm.

We sat on the wall to await his return, and it was minutes before we saw him coming in with the dead bird in his mouth. He came slowly, hesitatingly, one laggard foot after the other, as though undecided whether or not he was doing the proper thing.

While he was yet some forty feet away he stopped and surveyed us thoughtfully.

"Fetch," Gene called sharply, and he came on again.

We had risen from the wall and were standing with a distance of a dozen feet between us. The dog came in and paused once more before us. His eyes were troubled, and we watched with interest to see what he would do. He looked at his master intently, for a time, then came over and placed the bird definitely and decisively at my feet. With that gesture he turned, went quickly to his master, and stood beside him. His action said, as plainly as words—

"There's your bird. Whether you were right or wrong in killing him I do not know, but remember, you were the one who did the shooting. If any trouble arises from it, my boss isn't going to be blamed. It's your bird. Take it and do anything you like with it."

Good old Count! That was his first pheasant, but not his last. Never again, however, did he drop one at my feet.

He was a bold dog and afraid of no bodily harm. No thorn or brier patch ever deflected him from his course, and icy water was a thing he seemed to love. He would point any wild animal as staunchly as though it were a grouse, and feared no living thing.

No living thing? I wonder.

We were hunting Forgotten Land. It had been a settlement once, a century or more ago. There was evidence that the land had been cleared, but the forest had crept back and now all but hid the once fertile fields. Scattered about over the many hundreds of acres, were many almost obliterated cellar holes, and occasionally one came across the rotting remains of a crude farm wagon. Thoughts of the former occupants of the land kept intruding upon my mind. With the sweat of their brows they had wrested this soil from the clutch of the forest. With infinite exertion they had builded their homes on the sunny slopes. They had lived and loved and died and were dust again. Dust! Their homes were dust, and timber was growing in the once fallow fields.

It was a cheerless place in which to hunt, but there were hundreds of wild apple trees scattered about and it was good grouse country.

We had bagged several birds and had wandered into a part of the territory with which we were unfamiliar. We had passed through an open glade, a pleasant little Eden with an October sun shining on it, and had come to a higher bit of level ground on which a few scattering birches grew. Behind that was a heavy growth of pine.

I had just noticed the remains of another old cellar in the center of the plot when Count swung in a long cast before me and came to a sudden, startled halt. It was a likely place for grouse, but as I swung my gun free, something in the dog's attitude arrested my attention. He was not pointing, but he stood there in rigorous immobility, staring ahead toward the dark and gloomy pines.

Even as I gazed I saw the hackle on his back rise straight up until it stood four inches high. He stood thus for a moment, then, turning, tucked his tail tightly between his legs, and, with many a nervous backward glance, ran, fear-rid-den, to his master.

Instinctively we moved closer together and looked at each other. Then, by common consent, we slid the safeties off our guns and moved forward. Suddenly the sun's face was covered by a drifting cloud, and, in that instant, Count howled from somewhere in the rear, a long drawn, tremulous wolf howl such as his breed had not uttered for generations.

Determinedly we went on, but the place seemed unaccountably dark and dreary. There were no signs of life or movement, no telltale footprints on the ground. Nothing unusual that human eyes might discern. Nothing in the least unusual, with the exception of a narrow, rectangular mound of earth, its contours softened by the summer rains and winter snows of many years. A narrow mound of earth and nothing more. I do not fear the unknown. I am merely curious. I would give much to know what Count saw that day, in that forgotten corner of Forgotten Land, that caused him to run, with his tail between his legs, like a frightened, yellow cur.

To kill two flying grouse with one shot is a rare occur-rence. It has never been my luck to do it, on anything but ducks, but I have known authentic cases where it has happened, and was with Gene one day when he thought, for a minute or two, he had accomplished the unusual feat.

We had come from a thickly wooded covert into a pasture in which only a few scattering birches grew. Directly before us grew a dozen or more, stretching directly ahead in an almost perfectly straight line. The dog came to a staunch point some forty feet away and near the end of the young trees. Gene and I were side by side, but at the dog's point, I stepped over to the other side of the row of birches in order that we might, together, have a clear field of vision. That little detour left me to the right of, and about three steps behind, my companion. I had just reached the vantage point of my choosing when a pair of grouse flushed, simultaneously and close to the dog. One swung a little to the left, and I knew she would give Gene a clear shot. The other went straightaway, and I swung the gun on her. From the corner of my eye I saw Gene go into action, each movement synchronized with mine. The two guns cracked as one, and I saw my bird, her left wing broken and her body otherwise damaged, swing over into the path of the other falling bird.

There was a moment of intense silence, and then his voice arose, as exultant as a choir boy's on Easter morning, invoking eternal disaster upon himself if he had not killed two birds with one shot. I let him know the sweet glory of it for a few minutes and then asked what he supposed happened to the bird I shot at.

"Did you shoot?" he asked in surprise. "I didn't hear it."

I have always regretted my slow wittedness. Had I remained silent on that occasion he might have added a pleasing anecdote to the vast collection he has stored up for that day when he sits by the fire, with a shawl about his shoulders, and relates them, toothlessly, one by one, to his admiring grandchildren.

With pleasure I recall an incident when I was as surprised as he at the result of my shooting. I was back again in the enchanted Dead River country, seeking a rendezvous with a buck I had met the previous fall. I had come to a territory particularly barren of deer signs, and consequently received my customary thrill when I saw a grouse thrust its head from behind the base of a giant spruce some thirty feet away and peer at me with an inquisitive and beady eye.

The camp larder was low, so I took careful aim and pulled the trigger. With the report the bird quickly withdrew its head, and a moment later peeped out at me from the other side of the tree.

Again I shot, being careful to make no second mistake, and again it dodged back behind the massive bole. I jacked another shell into the chamber and waited. This time it stepped boldly out and my bullet decapitated it as cleanly as a farmer's hatchet could have done.

Disgusted with the thorough rottenness of my shooting, I went in to pick it up. Unfortunate and ill-fated bird to come to such an untimely end. It is said that misery loves company, yet I am sure it derived no consolation from the fact that two other grouse lay dead on the ground beside it.

An old storekeeper in a little town in Southern Maine gave me a bit of advice which I shall always remember, even if I, with my natural stubbornness, fail to profit by it.

I had driven fifty miles to hunt a woodcock covert which I had found quite by accident. It was, and still is, a glorious feeding ground for the "little russet feller" and well worth the time necessarily spent in reaching it.

We had started before daylight that morning and, in the last minute of confusion, I had delved in the shell case and extracted a box of duck loads rather than the 9's I invariably use for woodcock.

Discovering my mistake as we reached our destination, I drove on a few miles to a little town, in which there was a store that advertised ammunition. I went in, hoping for the best but expecting nothing smaller than 8's.

A gray-bearded octogenarian arose from behind the

counter as I entered, the rickety chair creaking in sympathy with his rusty joints.

"Yes, sir," he addressed me. "What can we do for you this morning?"

"I would like a box of woodcock loads," I answered. "Twelve gauge, loaded with either 9's or 10's."

"Woodcock loads?" He seemed bewildered. "Man, there ain't been a woodcock in this town, to my knowledge, for more than twenty years."

"I found one here last fall," I corrected him. "The last of the Mohicans. I missed him and thought I'd like to hunt him up again this year."

"Well, I'm supprised. So you seen a woodcock, eh? Well, well, well! Didn't suppose they was one left in the State of Maine. Be you sure it was a woodcock?"

I told him I was quite certain it was. It resembled that elusive bird as I remembered him. Did he have either 9's or 10's?

"I riccolect buyin' some 10's once fer a feller used to be here in town. Kind of a taxidermist he was. Used to stuff birds. Ordered some 10's fer him to shoot hummin' birds with. Don't know's he ever got any."

From the car outside came the whine of an impatient dog. I tried to put firmness in my tone. "Have you any fine shot?"

[182]

"Five's," he informed me, "is the smallest we carry. Double B's for foxes, 2's for ducks, and 5's for pa'tridge and squirrels. Them's the right sizes I callate."

I had neither the time nor inclination for argument. My one desire was to efface myself gracefully without giving offense. I told him I had determined to try 9's that fall, and unless something busted, I would do it.

"Young feller," he said, "I'm older'n you be, and I'd like to give ye some advice. If ye want to kill birds, an' I s'pose ye do or ye wouldn't be huntin' em, get a full choke gun with a good long barrel, load her with 5's and see what happens. When a bird gits up, p'int the gun right at her;" he went through the motions carefully, swinging, with left arm extended and right elbow raised, in a cumbersome arc that embraced half the store; "p'int it the same as you would a rifle and you'll kill 'em a damn long ways off."

My hand was on the door knob. I turned it and, pulling gently inward, felt the crisp October air engulf me.

"You have the distance figured correctly," I told him, and went out and closed the door.

CHAPTER X

EVEN while I have been writing this a change has taken place around me. The Master Painter has been at work, and the leaves outside my window, which but a short time ago were a verdant, emerald green, are now a riot of blazing color. Crimson and brown and gold, they flaunt their exquisite beauty before my eyes. It is fall again. The chestnut burrs have opened with the first hard frost and are spilling their mahogany-hued fruit upon the cool, damp earth. The wild grapes have ripened and the apples are beginning to fall. There is a tang in the morning air and the blood tingles in my veins.

It is grouse time again. I need no calendar to tell me that. The old drummer has found his log and the staccato beat of his wings is audible in the stillness of the October afternoon. The woodcock have begun their long migration, and the fall ducks are in. The red gods are calling and I must go.

I wonder, sometimes, if I am duly appreciative of the good fortune that has been mine. In all probability I am not. Too few of us really are. But I have much to be thankful for. I am glad that, from a space so infinite and vast that no human mind can begin to conceive its magnitude, those little molecules of dust were assembled into the composite body that is myself. I am glad to be alive. I have tasted life and I have found it sweet.

I am thankful for a certain measure of good health; for an appetite that makes my mouth water at the sight of a yearling steer, and for digestive organs which would not balk at the task of assimilating it. I adore my little family, I love my many friends, and I am happy to know that the things which thrilled me in my youth still hold all the old attractions.

Yesterday I went hunting with Bill. For some years I have had my first hunt of the season with him. We make quite a rite of it, a sort of gala day, and it is right that it is so, for Bill has been my lifelong friend and was one of the mentors of my youth. Older than I, his woodcraft and grouse lore was, and still is, superior to mine, and much of the little I know about shooting is directly attributable to him. I left before the dawn and was in the territory I knew, in those halcyon days of my youth, in time to see the eastern skies crimson over the Atlantic.

Hallowed ground those coverts are to me, and as I come to them, one by one, memories rise, as unbidden as the morning mists, and engulf me.

In the hollow, just back of that hill, is the little pond to which I crawled one day when, because of the force of a terrific nor'easter, crawling was the easiest form of locomotion. There, with the last bit of cover some sixty yards from the pool, I gazed out, striving to keep my eyes open against the wind and stinging rain, and saw the little pool filled, to the last available inch, with black ducks. I looked long at my little 20 gauge and the intervening distance ere I, youthful game hog that I was, took a pot shot at them with both barrels. Incredible as it may sound, a few scattering ducks hurtled up into that gigantic wind, but the main flock, fully fifty in number, rested without motion on that little pool.

With bulging eyes I started forth to reap the greatest harvest of ducks ever garnered since the days of the Pilgrim Fathers, but had taken only a step when they went up as a single unit and I, with empty gun, watched them depart. It was minutes before I came to understand that the report of the gun was so distorted and torn asunder by that inconceivable wind that it caused them practically no alarm at a distance of only sixty yards.

There is an alder run where I found Gleam, a five months setter pup, pointing a grouse. The surprising thing was that I had hunted for her for a half hour and, when I found her, she was sitting back on her haunches, with fatigue, but she had the grouse nailed like a veteran.

I invoke a bad, bad word upon distemper. Gleam had

all that heart could desire. Her blood was of the bluest and she had a remarkable amount of inherited bird sense. No ordinary amount of money would have taken her from me, but I lost her and, for a time, the days seemed gloomy and long.

It was here we killed the first—and last—fox ahead of the first—and last—fox hound I ever, even jointly, owned. We had parted, three of us, with five slowly accumulated dollars, solely because of the masterly salesmanship of a be-whiskered farmer who owned him. He, Ananias that he was, vowed, as Heaven was his witness, that "that dog will run a fox all day long in a circle a half-mile square." So long as we owned him, never again did he find a fox in a circle of that rather uncommon shape, while for a fox in an oval or even slightly elliptic circle he held the utmost contempt.

We mourned the loss of the five dollars, but it was with a sigh of vast relief that we slipped the collar from his neck, just outside his own dooryard, and bade him Godspeed and a last, long good-bye.

Down that lane is where "Lammy" and I found the den in which Emil Harab, the skunk, lived with his harem. We dug him out, the old reprobate, and gained mightily by doing so. The sum total of our profits from that venture was something like six dollars, in cash, for the eight hides; a profound knowledge of—and an equally profound respect for —skunk anatomy; a gloriously unexpected three-day vacation from school, and a B. O. which even Lifebuoy could not conquer.

Well! Who would have thought that possible? What a change in a few short years! Twenty years ago this country, at my right, was a barren stripped lot, and now it is crowded with thrifty young pines. It was here that peppy little Dick, the sweetest cow pony ever foaled in New England, gave me the outstanding ride of my life. Dick and I used to haze the cows to pasture in the morning and home again at night. He came, in time, to understand that the proper place for cows and frivolous young stock was in the well worn trail we followed. If one of the herd ventured from it, he made it his immediate business to put her back exactly where she belonged. If the creature chanced to be optimistic enough to believe she could outrun him, she was speedily convinced of her mistake. With ears laid back and teeth clicking like castanets, he would tear down on her like a whirlwind and speedily convince her of her indiscretion. He was a wise little horse and I suppose he came to believe nothing with four legs and a tail could outrun him. He learned, however, that he was in error.

[189]

It was deer hunting time and Brad and I had our deer spotted; a lazy old doe, a pair of fawns and a magnificent buck. They were staying in a little swamp that was less than a quarter mile from the road. When jumped, they followed a pine ridge out to the road, crossed it, and entered the cut-off at the left. It was thickly dotted with pine stumps and brush-piles, affording excellent cover for a standing deer, but one in motion could be seen for a half mile.

Brad and I had driven up, in a light spring wagon. I had dropped him around the bend several hundred yards back. The plan was for him to cut in to the rear of the swamp and drive the deer out. I would be waiting where the pine ridge met the road. Heigh-ho! It was a perfect plan. We even had the horse and wagon with which to cart them home.

Jogging slowly up to the stand, it occurred to me that it might be an excellent idea to shoot from the wagon. Dick was not gunshy, and the chances were that the sight and smell of a horse would frighten no deer. There was a slight rise of ground about thirty yards from the pine ridge and here we halted. I turned Dick slightly so that he faced the cutoff, thereby giving myself plenty of sea room in the event a bombardment ensued.

We waited. Five minutes—ten minutes. Then, from near at hand, a rifle crashed, once—twice—thrice—and, almost instantly thereafter, that old buck leaped across the road within twenty feet of us. No following the pine ridge for him. He was going places and he chose the line of least resistance. I leaped to my feet and swung the gun toward him and, in that instant, Dick laid his ears back and went into action with the disconcerting suddenness of a released catapult.

"Doggone your hide!" he said. "Get back in the road where you belong or I'll bite your ears off."

By the merest fraction of an inch, and by a miracle of balance, I saved myself from going backward over the seat. Clutching desperately at whatever offered a handhold, I saved myself, momentarily, and reached for the reins which were wound about the whip socket. Then a wheel hit a stump. I went into the air like a released balloon and came down, on my stomach, across the seat. Rolling over, I reached for the reins once more, but it was not to be. We went over a brush-pile and the wagon tilted like a banking plane. I grasped the back of the seat to save myself and heard the sickening screech of a screw tearing loose from the tortured wood beneath me. With a lurch we came to a level keel once more, only to lean more perilously in the other direction.

Fleeting moments there were when I caught photographic glimpses of the old buck splitting the wind before us, and of little Dick, with ears laid back, running magnificently behind him. The wagon was a handicap but he disregarded it and gave his last full ounce of energy to the task of heading that fleeing phantom, while I clung desperately to the rifle, with one hand, and to the fast loosening seat with the other.

The ending was inevitable. I had visualized it long seconds before, with all the anticipatory nerve tingle of an air pilot, dropping earthward with a defective 'chute. It came quickly, like a lightning flash, yet it was ages long. Time is the greatest of prevaricators. Winged hours of bliss speed by in the briefest of seconds, while seconds of suspense drag on through eternity.

We hit a decayed log and caromed from it to a prodigious pine stump. Like a drowning man grasping a straw, I clutched the rifle and seatback yet more desperately as we sailed out into infinite space. I recall seeing the blue sky beneath me and the brown earth above, as I achieved a mid-air somersault which approached perfection. Then—O miracle of miracles—I alighted, on my feet—running. I did not go down and neither did I drop the tightly held rifle in my right hand nor the wagon seat in my left.

Little Dick must have sensed my hurried departure instantly, for he suddenly slid to a stiff-legged stop and looked back questioningly at me. It may be that he realized how hopelessly outclassed he was, and welcomed this opportunity to give over the chase. I placed the seat on its broken supports and climbed in, whereupon the wise little horse turned, of his own accord, and picked his way, carefully and sedately, back to the road once more.

Ah, yes, 'tis hallowed ground, but where once my leaden feet pursued the weary, homeward way, I now flit past, without exertion, at forty miles an hour. Bill was waiting on the front steps, a shapely young pointer posing beside him. Bill has passed the fifty mark, but he came out to the car with the old, deceptive stride. He toes in slightly as a woodsman should, and he is split nearly to his Adam's apple. His dark eyes retain all their old brightness, and his hair is still thick and dark and wavy.

The years have dealt kindly with him, and, barring accident, he will still be hunting grouse at eighty. I noted, with satisfaction, the dog was watching his every move with adoring eyes. All Bill's dogs have been like that. They place him on a throne, and he sees that they keep him there. I went in the house and shook the hand of Mrs. Bill, and drank a cup of glorious coffee while Bill donned his shooting coat and methodically counted the shells it contained.

"There's one advantage in present day hunting," he observed. "A chap can travel considerable lighter than he could in the old days. Imagine starting off with only seventeen shells. I've shot that many in an hour when I was a youngster."

"You may do it again, sometime, Bill."

He shook his head in a decided negative.

"Never," he said with finality. "They'll never be that plentiful again, and if they were, I wouldn't care to shoot that much in one hour—or one day."

"Why? Is your shoulder getting tender with the advancing years?"

"Not my shoulder," Bill answered, "but my conscience. No matter how plentiful grouse become again, I'll never kill as many as I did in the old days. My viewpoint has changed since then. I get a lot more fun from watching the work of the dog, and am satisfied with two or three birds for the day."

I rejoiced that Bill had come to my way of thinking. Getting in the car, I swung it about and headed for a covert that was our favorite in the old days.

It is still a sweetheart, and I thrilled with anticipation as we entered it. To the north is rising ground which, despite the ravages of predatory lumbermen, is still heavily wooded with pine. To the left is a mile of unbroken swamp land in which blueberry bushes and trailing blackberry vines abound. Between the swamp and the higher ground lies a hundred or more acres of sprout land on a springy, southern slope. Here the grouse love to lie after their morning feed in the swamp. If we flush them in the morning, they invariably fly into the pine growth, but will be back again in an hour or more. If the birds are here, we spend the entire day in this one covert and find in the afternoon the same birds which we missed in the morning.

Bill strapped a bell about the dog's neck and said, "All right, boy, go get 'em."

He went, at express train speed, and we grinned and watched him, knowing that some of that excess vitality must be worked off before he could steady down to the business of the day.

From a distance came the sound of a grouse taking wing, then another, and another, followed in swift succession. The young pointer had put them up which, in an old dog, is an unpardonable fault.

"Three of 'em," said Bill. "He's wild as a parson's daughter, for the first half hour. He'll never be the dog Sport was."

"Sport had more birds killed over his points than this youngster will probably ever see. That makes a mighty big difference."

"Sure," agreed Bill. "A dog would get as much experience in a week, then, as he can possibly obtain in an entire season now. Ah! there you are, you young tornado. What do you mean by flushing those birds? What do you think your nose is for, anyway? Go on, now, and use a little common sense."

The pointer seemed to sense the reproof in Bill's voice, for he started off again at reduced speed. Suddenly he stopped and, with head held high, sniffed the wind before him. Then, with infinite caution, his questing nose quivering with the scent of game, he advanced slowly.

It matters not how often I see that action repeated; to me it will always be a miracle.

Two powerful forces are at work within the dog: the age-old, inherited instinct to course the quarry; and the newer instinct, man-made, to stalk and point the bird. By careful, selective breeding man has achieved a process of evolution, in only a few hundred years, which nature might well have taken thousands to equal.

Stepping lightly, the pointer worked in and paused momentarily, his body stiffening anxiously as he did so. Relaxing, he moved on a score of feet, slower and slower with each inch of ground gained, then stopped and became as rigid as a thing of bronze.

I had seen thousands of just such poses, yet, as always, I paused to drink in the beauty of it, and saw Bill give me an appraising glance.

"Great stuff," I whispered. Bill grinned and motioned

to the right. By that wordless sign I knew he wished me to get where I could intercept the bird, should she break toward the pine growth. Accordingly, I made a quick detour and came back some thirty yards ahead and to the right of the dog, and climbed up on an old stump.

"O. K.," I said, and heard Bill move immediately in toward the dog.

"Whir-r-r-r!" A grouse came out through the low bushes, straight for my head. A perfect shot, but Bill and the dog were back there somewhere, directly in line. But this is old stuff. I know the answer ere the bird has covered half the distance that separates us. Right-about-face, quickly, and take her after she goes over your head; a perfect, straightaway shot.

I pivoted on the rotten stump and, as I did so, half of it disintegrated and one foot slid off. Regaining my balance, I swung the gun to my shoulder, only to see the bird vanish behind a low evergreen some thirty yards away. One lost second and no more but, oh, what a difference it makes when swinging on a grouse that is well under way!

"What's the matter out there?" called Bill. "Had a stroke of some kind?"

"Yeah. A stroke of misfortune," I answered. "I'm too good at this game. Figured to an inch where she would go and then, like an idiot, stood exactly there."

"Watch out!" This from Bill. "Another point! I'll put her out to—"

"Whir-r-r-r!" In exactly the same groove, another grouse came, bullet-like, toward me. Turning my back to her I threw the gun to my shoulder and was ready when she went hurtling past. The thing is ridiculously easy when the turn is executed before the bird reaches one. She crumpled in the air and came down without a wing beat.

"That's hitting 'em," said Bill. "Let the pup find her. I'm teaching him to retrieve. Steady, boy. Dead bird! Fetch!"

With head high, he located the bird without difficulty and pointed staunchly. I like to see a young dog do that. It is a mark of steadiness and dependability and is pretty good evidence that his brain cavity is not packed with sawdust.

Bill held him steady for a moment, then sent him on. He went in and picked the bird up promptly, without mouthing it, and brought it proudly out.

Number one! What a comfortable feeling it is to slide the first bird into one's coat soon after entering a covert. The sun shines warmer, while the wood fairies whisper that this is to be the day you have dreamed of so long, when every bird in the woods will seek you out and fly directly before you, in the open and well within range.

We moved on. The dog, coursing before us, became

momentarily cautious, then loosened up and quartered over to the left. Bill swung over that way and I, returning the gun to the hollow of my arm, from whence it had involuntarily emerged at the dog's warning, plodded ahead over the ground the dog had covered, carelessly confident that no grouse would flush unexpectedly here.

"Whir-r-r-r!"

Oh, what a shock to the nervous system as that bird zoomed skyward from a distance of less than a score of feet. My arms seemed leaden as I tried to get into action. The bird was swinging sharply to the left, the gun was cuddled to my cheek, and I was swinging on him fast when I saw him crumple in mid-air, a split second before the report of Bill's gun hit my eardrums.

Instantly I heard him calling the dog in. "Drop!" he said. "Drop—and stay there. If you can't smell 'em alive you don't get a whiff after they're dead." He went in and picked up the bird. "He'll never be the dog his daddy was," he said to me. "Came near stepping on that one, didn't he?"

"Pretty close to it," I admitted, "but the best of them miss one sometimes."

"Sport didn't miss 'em."

"Sport was one of those once-in-a-lifetime dogs, Bill. It's hardly fair to compare this youngster with that old veteran. Ten years from now you'll be telling another pup

what a good dog this one was, and Sport will be but a forgotten dream."

"Maybe," said Bill, but he was silent and thoughtful as
we trailed the energetic young pointer.

"It seems kind of tough to forget—and be forgotten,"
he said then, "but I guess it is better so. I'll learn to be content. That's a likely youngster and he'll make a dog good
enough for me to finish out the game with. He'll never be
as good as I could make him if the birds were like they used
to be—but they ain't—and perhaps that's just as well, too.

"I remember coming home one night with seventeen
grouse, eight woodcock and two jack rabbits; a backload
of game—and the most I ever killed in one day. But what
was the sense of it? I could shoot well enough, then, so that
I was sure of every decently open shot. That took all the
sporting chance away. I didn't need the game. Had to give
it away to neighbors who, oftentimes, weren't particularly
fussy about getting it. All the time, I was getting my fun
out of watching the work of the dog, and wasn't bright
enough to know it. I've been pretty much of a fool all my
life, I guess."

"But we've found happiness, Bill. 'Where ignorance is
bliss, 'tis folly to be wise.' If I were beginning all over again,
I would follow pretty much the same trail. Wouldn't you?"

"Practically," he admitted. "But I'd use more discretion the second time. Oh—Oh! There's a picture for you. How's that for a snappy point?"

We ate our lunch in the glorious October sunshine, in a riot of blazing color. What an added zest it gives to the plainest of foods. Then too, we had that comfortable, satisfied feeling that two men may know when they each have a pair of grouse in their shooting coats at noontime. The day cannot be spoiled now. We have birds enough, and the afternoon is in the laps of the gods. If they choose to be bountiful, we will accept their offerings gratefully; if they withhold their largess, we are still content.

We rested for an hour ere we started back, for midday hunting has always been unproductive.

With the subject of shooting uppermost in my mind I asked, "Have you made many doubles in recent years, Bill?"

"No. The thing isn't as common as some people think. When we used to drive 'em up in bunches of a half dozen it wasn't much of a trick to take one with each barrel, but the chance comes pretty seldom now. I made one last year, the only chance I had."

"I count that only a double when both birds get into the air simultaneously, don't you, Bill?"

"Absolutely," he said. "If there's an instant's difference

in the time of rising, it is merely two singles. A good clean double is a pretty fast thing to pull off, on grouse. And that reminds me of something I've always wanted to see done."

"What is that?" I asked.

"I've always wanted to see four birds rise simultaneously and within easy range when I had a good man with me. That's asking too much, I suppose, but, just once, I'd like to see a double double. Did you ever hear of its being done?"

"Not on grouse, or woodcock either, now that I stop and think. But it's too late in the century, old man, to have dreams like that. You should have thought of that twenty-five years ago. It can't happen now."

"I suppose not," sighed Bill. "All the same, I'd like to see the opportunity presented. I'd like to see it happen to-day with you and me within fifteen yards when they rose. I'd like to know if I could do my part."

"Well, let's get after them," I suggested. "Today may be the day you have dreamed about all your life. Who knows?"

"That's one of the most interesting things about this game," said Bill. "Something entirely new happens almost every day you are in the woods. You think you have learned the last trick in the bag and then they pull a new one on you. O. K. partner. We're going after 'em!"

The homeward way we chose was a route closer to the big swamp than we had taken on the way in. It was a good rabbit country, and the young dog pointed one before we had gone a hundred yards.

"I wish he wouldn't do that," Bill fumed. "I get all fussed up, expecting a grouse to rise, and then a jack rabbit bounds out of a brush-pile."

"Most young dogs do it. It's game and the scent holds them up. He will learn the difference in time."

"Yes, and before he learns it, I'll have walked my legs off. I know what to do to cure him; just walk off and leave him on point. Let him know I'm not interested in rabbits at all. The heck of it is, however, to know when it's a rabbit."

Not less than three times in the next hour the pup repeated the offense. Bill was disgusted. "It breaks down my morale," he said. "I'm getting so that I expect every point will produce a cottontail. The next time he does that we'll sneak off and let him point until he gets tired of it. That'll teach him something."

The next point, it happened, was on grouse, and Bill made one of his old-time Annie Oakley shots that I can never hope to equal. The bird rose behind a low evergreen which hid her from view, but she chose another for her protecting screen on the getaway. She had not an inch over fifteen feet to go to gain sanctuary, but she failed to make it, and good, accurate old Bill had a foot or two to spare.

"You're getting pretty old and feeble, aren't you?" I asked, and Bill grinned his slow, quiet smile.

"I just naturally had to speed up on that one," he said, "but it put a crick in my back doing it. I wish I was twenty years old again."

"You never pulled a shot like that when you were twenty, Bill. That is something that requires experience, and plenty of it."

"Well, I've had plenty," Bill answered, "and so have you. If we had been even half bright, we would have been the world's champions instead of a pair of second raters. There goes that fool dog again after another rabbit. Dog-gone his hide. This time he can stay there and point till he can't stand up, for all I care. Come on. Don't pay any attention to him."

I took a few reluctant steps, then paused.

"How do you know it's a rabbit?" I asked.

"Couldn't you see?" snapped Bill. "Didn't you notice how high headed he went in, and the wiggle in the tip of his tail? When you see him do that, it's a rabbit every time."

"Just the same," I said, "I don't like to go off and leave him that way. Mind if I look?"

"Not at all," he answered. "Go to it."

[204]

I went in boldly, confidently, with the gun under my arm. Bill was right, of course. Bill knew his dogs as other men do their children. "A pretty point, that, and a nice looking dog, too. Wish I had the camera along. Pretty open country, here. That rabbit must lie in the brush-heap. No other cover to speak of. Well, I'll kick it and watch him sail out in high gear."

I took a step ahead, and, with a disconcerting roar, four grouse took wing simultaneously from the farther edge of the brush-pile, and less than ten yards distant. Straightaway they went in a perfect fan formation. Bill could never have dreamed of a more ideal opportunity than this.

I slipped the gun from under my arm and covered the right-hand bird. She was less than twenty yards away and an easy, open shot, but my finger did not tighten on the trigger. I slid the gun back and turned to the dog.

"Speaking for myself, I apologize humbly," I said. "I was a triple-plated fool but, at that, I was a prodigy compared to your master. Before he gets here I'd like to tell you that the uncomplimentary remarks he has made, concerning the gray matter in your head, are now a thing of the past. Good old Bill has made the mistake of his life."

"How many were there?" Bill asked as he came up behind us.

"Four."

"Close?"

"About ten yards. Nice open shooting. Corking place for a double double."

"Why didn't you shoot?"

"Without you? Take one bird out of that perfect foursome? I think not."

"I think I'd like to go home," said Bill. "I have a new neighbor, a big, husky two hundred pounder. He's sort of simple, but he'll do exactly as he is told. I'm going to hire him to kick me around his door yard for precisely thirty minutes."

I am home again. I have driven back in the starlight, over those well-remembered, old-time trails. There is a white frost in the lowlands, and a new moon peeps at me over my right shoulder. I am not really superstitious, but enough so that I know this to be a good omen.

Why shouldn't it be? It is the woodcock moon. By its silvery light they will start their long migration, and our coverts are in their line of flight. I anticipate much from them.

The grouse, too, will soon be seeking the old apple orchards, and scores of these are encircled with red on my personal map.

I am tired, deliciously tired, but I know a great content.

I sit by the fire, living over again the events of the day. Bob is lying at my feet, his soft brown eyes gazing up into mine beseechingly. I know of what he is thinking. I gather up my manuscript and answer the dog's unspoken question.

"Yes, boy, we're going, tomorrow."